CHOOSE STRONG

"THE CHOICE THAT CHANGES EVERYTHING"

WRITTEN BY:

SALLY MCRAE

Book Cover Designed by: Alex Rodriguez
Cover Photo/Bio Photo by: Tyler McCain

Dedicated to:

my love, Eddie James
&
my greatest gifts,
Makenzie Diane & Isaiah James

THIS BOOK CHANGES LIVES

Because of your purchase, orphans and
those in need will be helped.
Every year, *Sally McRae Inc.* donates thousands
of dollars in an effort to assist non-profit
organizations working directly with those in the most
vulnerable situations. Whether you download my Strength
App, purchase a KYHU product, subscribe to my YouTube
channel, or purchase my books, know that you are helping.
Caring for orphans, widows, and the impoverished is
vital, so I want to thank you for your kindness. To learn
more about the non-profit organizations I donate to,
please scan the QR code in the back of this book or visit
sallymcrae.com

CHOOSE STRONG

"THE CHOICE THAT
CHANGES EVERYTHING"

WRITTEN BY:
SALLY MCRAE

CONTENTS

FOREWORD

By: Nick Bare

L ife is hard. You will experience the highest of highs and the lowest of lows. Sometimes it feels like you're climbing a mountain and taking the hit of a headwind for miles - just like an ultra. But no matter how hard it gets, how much resistance accumulates, and how much your mind and body are begging you to stop, choose strong.

I'm honored to have a small part in this book that shares the trials and tribulations of one of the strongest individuals I've ever met. The first time I heard of Sally McRae was after she won the Badwater 135 in 2021. The Badwater Ultramarathon is a 135-mile race from Death Valley to Mt. Whitney, deemed the world's toughest foot race. Completing a 100+ mile race requires much grit, pain, and perseverance, but taking the women's field on such a respected course demands strength and strength beyond physical ability. Sally and I had mutual friends, and everyone I knew had described her in a way that I can only categorize as a humble warrior. After getting to know Sally on a more personal level, sitting down and talking about our childhoods, the impact our mothers had on our lives before passing, and the reason we both chose the path of most resistance over the years leading up to today, I knew she was someone that I needed in my life. You will learn a lot about Sally in this book, including experiences that shaped the person she is today, but it's not meant to spotlight her successes and hardships. It will provide you with a reason for being strong and courageous. It will instill purpose in the decisions you make that guide the life that you want to live. Embrace every aspect of these stories because they are lessons shared to make us stronger.

There is an unpopular opinion about "hard," and the truth is - it's all relative. What is easy for you now was hard at some point in your past. What is hard for you now should be easier for you at some point in the future. That's growth, and growth is a choice. It's never by chance. From someone who thrives in a challenge, building from the ground up and starting from scratch, I know these humbling moments strengthen me. That is why I (and if you are reading this book, I can assume you do as well) choose strong. The first time I met Sally in person was for a podcast recording. She flew into Austin, Texas, on a late flight, and we spent two hours locked in a room discussing her life journey of the previous four decades. We skipped over the surface-level conversations and dove deep into life, death, purpose, and pain. I'm a person who feeds off others' energy, passion, and drive - Sally was exploding in all. I could feel what she had been through and visualize her direction. When someone's vision is so clear, after a past of being very blurry, they are unstoppable. It was after the first time meeting Sally that I knew she was someone special.

We are born pure and innocent. Nothing had molded our character as a newborn. You'll learn through Sally's story that everything we have experienced, heard, tried, tested, failed, succeeded, or felt guided the person we have become at this moment in time. The sum of Sally's decisions throughout her life has led her to where she is today. The same goes for you and me.

And the person we are right now might be different than who we become five, ten, or fifteen years from today. That's growth - for better or worse. It's easy to blame your childhood, parents, lack of opportunities, or sub-par natural talent as the reason you aren't where you want to be today. But to choose strong, we must choose the hard right over the easy wrong. Those "weaknesses" become strengths. They are a competitive advantage built on the foundation of resilience. Hardships sharpen us. Discomfort sharpens us. The greater the repetition, the sharper we get.

Knowing Sally has changed the way I view my life's purpose. She isn't pushing her body to its physical limits to prove anyone wrong - she does it to prove herself right. No matter how bad it gets and how heavy it may feel, there is always an opportunity to grow and choose strong. "Choosing strong" takes practice and requires repetition. With consistency, choosing strong becomes easier. It becomes the only way through. Choosing to be strong is physical, mental, and emotional. It's all part of the journey. Thank you, Sally, for sharing yours.

Nick Bare
Founder & CEO of Bare Performance Nutrition,
US Army Infantry Veteran, and Author of "25 Hours A Day"

DON'T SKIP THIS PAGE!

D id it work? The above title... well you're still reading so that's a win. Most people skip the prologue and go straight to Chapter One— admittedly, that's what I used to do, but after a bit of guidance and research, I learned how valuable these next paragraphs will be to you, so hang with me for a few minutes.

I imagine there's two types of readers who will initially pick up my book— there is the crowd who knows me on social media as @yellowrunner and then there's the community where I've existed for over a decade as a professional ultra runner, "Sally McRae, the one with big quads who lifts weights and laughs really loud." (*Not my quote*) If you don't know me from either of those places, maybe you picked up this memoir because the cover was cool(*Thanks to Alex Rodriguez and Tyler McCain.*) However you arrived here, I want to thank you—- it took me twenty years to finish this book.

Fear slowed the process of completing this book. That may come as a surprise because I often stand before audiences or share in interviews about being strong and courageous. An important part of my career involves overcoming fear. There might be the expectation that the following chapters will be about running or my unconventional ways of strength training, so spoiler alert-*that* is not what this book is about.

So what will **YOU** get out of reading this book? My greatest hope is that you finish this book *stronger than when you started*. We all have a story to tell and I believe every story is important... that's another thing I hope you harness by the time you turn the final page, *belief in YOUR story*. Belief holds great power in your life and what you believe to be true of yourself has the ability to empower or destroy you—- which is why I'm sharing my story with you.

The first 18 years of my life almost destroyed me. It was an ultra long season of battling abuse, fear, pain, self-hate, and earth-shattering loss. It's important for you to know that some of these memories are so delicate that I do not use the names or actual descriptions of anyone in my family except myself and my mother. The stories of my family members are for them alone to tell. I have also modified some of the dates, places, and names of people to further protect those involved.

One of the most asked questions of my running career is, **"How do you keep going?"** Over the years my answers to that question have been brief and to the point while other times, I have spent 30-40 minutes giving talks based entirely on the topic. But it isn't until now that I disclosed the *full* story of how I built a foundation of strength and learned to choose strong and keep going no matter the circumstance. Ultimately, my hope is that these stories will strengthen you; and encourage you no matter where you are in YOUR journey.

I'm not here to tell you how to live your life or tell you why you're failing in this or that. I'm not going to pretend that I'm anyone extraordinary— truthfully, I'm flawed, prideful and in need of grace.

There is one thing; however, that I will remind you repeatedly throughout the book:

You are Strong. As humans, we need truthful daily reminders amid the loud and sometimes faulty messages swirling around us. Strength is something you can stand on; and I hope as you turn the last page that you are stronger than when you first started reading this book. I know I already wrote that, but now you know its importance as you read through these pages.

You are strong.

I hope you choose to believe it.

I hope you choose to stand in it,

Unaltered and fully valid.

Your strong friend,

(yellowrunner)

CHAPTER 1

UNALTERED AND FULLY VALID

Dad threw mom on the floor when he found out she was pregnant. He screamed in her face and told her she did it on purpose. They were both nineteen years old. Despite the raging incident, Mom loved Dad, and it seemed to be the right thing to do—to marry the father of your unborn baby. Five months later, on a December day in 1974, Mama walked down the aisle with a tiny baby bump beneath her wedding dress and said, "I do."

I'm sure you can tell my family didn't get off to a great start. After Mama told me this story while I was still a teenager, I questioned why she married a man who hurt her. Mama lovingly pointed out, "Well, you wouldn't be here if I didn't marry him, so I believe it was a good thing." Although not satisfied with her response, her perspective softened me, impressing me with her endless ability to find light in even the darkest spaces. I think it's common to want someone like this in our life—someone brave enough to show us that good can come from even the most difficult situations.

Raised as an only child, Mama described herself as the shy girl with only a few friends in high school—opposite of Dad who was raised one of six children and popular among his peers. Dad was from a large Hollywood family. His father was successful in the film industry and his mom was a talented dancer, having appeared in black and white films where the characters sang and danced.

A musical genius, Dad could play several instruments by ear and even taught himself to play the guitar upside down after learning left-handed guitars didn't exist. His genuine passion was playing the drums and singing, and he was already performing in bands by the time he was in grade school. However, Mama telling him about the baby shattered his dream of becoming a famous musician, as he now felt compelled to focus on raising and providing for Mama and the baby.

Mama described those initial years of marriage as troubled. They separated from each other for a couple of years while Dad attempted to pursue his musical dreams, but he returned, and they worked through their struggles. Four years after my brother was born and within less than six years, Mama gave birth to four daughters. I am the middle of the five children.

Mama said I was her easiest labor and within four hours, my nine pound body was placed in her arms with a bald head and a smile. At eight months old, I started walking and by the time I was one, Mama chronicled in my baby book how I was a physically strong and passionate baby. She wrote that I enjoyed playing alone, often busying myself for long periods of time in quiet concentration. As the months passed and with each passing milestone, Mama documented my perpetual smile and curiosity as I engaged with people and the world around me. As I grew older, she called me her Little Bear and Sunshine.

We lived in the coastal city of Bonita Mesa, in California. The first house I remember was a small two-bedroom rental on a misplaced piece of land next to a loud, busy street. Finances were tight in the early years and although Mama wanted to live in an actual neighborhood, she did her best to make the small space our home. I shared a room with my four siblings—two bunk beds and a crib nestled into the four corners of a low-lit room with brown shaggy carpet and extra thick green curtains.

My earliest childhood memory happened in that house on Vista Drive—a dark reel of chaos that has played without warning in my mind throughout my life.

One evening in 1983, we sat down to eat in our small dining room. Sounds from the television filled the quiet and the fading sun pushed a few last rays through cracks in the screen door. The scene dimmed as Dad's voice erupted, "What is this slop? You call this dinner?"

Unable to comprehend Dad's agitation, my four-year-old self joined in the excitement, so I happily stood upon my chair and chimed, "Yeah, what is this stuff?"

My siblings stared at me with enormous eyes, and my baby sister started crying.

Let me pause here to point out a particular detail from this scene—the fact that I'm standing. Further in the book, I talk about the act of standing and how it marked pivotal points in my life. One of my favorite definitions of the word *stand* is "to remain valid or unaltered." Early on, I struggled to believe my life was valid, and I lived much of my life trying to alter who I was or what I showed others to separate myself from the pain I knew at home. Dozens of definitions and phrases about *standing* come to mind, such as "taking a stand or standing against." Whether literally or figuratively, standing holds immense power. As a young girl, I was now experimenting with that power in the most optimistic way. Even with Dad's harsh tone, I thought well of him and believed an exciting moment was about to start. Call me a typical middle child, or maybe just a kid who believed she was valid enough to stand. I stood upon my chair, unaltered, ready for what was next.

Dad, however, ignored me and continued with an intense tone, "And look at the house, you lazy bum! I work all day and come home to this?"

Fear gripped my breath as I watched the man who looked like Dad transform into a scary monster—or at least that's how my forming brain struggled to make sense of it. It was confusing that the man who sometimes surprised us on Sunday mornings with a pink box filled with donuts and who hugged Mama extra tight in the kitchen was the same man before me. This man was like one of the mean monsters in the cartoons I watched on TV. The monster who made the good guys run away with scared looks on their faces. Those monsters were ugly and their eyes were cold and scary. My dad was handsome, and when he smiled, his blue eyes smiled, too. But now, I couldn't see Dad—only a heaving figure with icy eyes and skin that was turning a deeper shade of red each time he yelled.

Mama scooped up my baby sister from the highchair and begged the monster to calm down, but it only made his rage more intense. I followed his odd body with my eyes, transfixed by how quickly he grabbed the nearby laundry basket with his paw. Mama hurried from the table, leaving us to watch the monster hurl the basket across the living room where she tried to get away. The sight of the basket flying made my mouth open and without warning, a giant breath of air rushed into my lungs. As if in slow motion, I watched the clothes Mama recently folded scatter onto the carpet. *Where was Daddy? What was that monster gonna do to my Mama?*

Searching for comfort, I scanned my siblings' scared faces and paralyzed bodies, which only made me feel out of place. Why was I still standing? Who was going to help Mama?

A sound like thunder exploded in the room as the monster punched his paw through the wall, snarling at Mama that it was her fault. My little heart jumped around in my chest—never had it beat with such force. The monster chased Mama into the bedroom and slammed the door, causing us to tremble in our seats.

We waited, weeping, as we listened to Mama pleading. My helplessness made my tummy hurt, and I wondered about my baby sister. I imagined Mama holding her small, curly blonde head against her chest, protecting her. I imagined Mama's tears rolling down from her warm brown eyes. Was she afraid, like me? The thoughts were unbearable, and I sank into my seat.

I remember no more from that night.

At a young age, I began learning important lessons for my journey ahead.

People can hurt others even if they love them.

Fear paralyzes and makes me feel powerless.

I learned standing took strength, and hopelessness made me weak.

I learned when Dad got angry, a monster appeared.

My journey was shaping into a confusing one, and without knowing it, I was cementing opinions about myself and the world around me. How did I navigate a life that was frightening?

I had a distinctive introduction to fear and as I grew, its power to steal my hope and make me sit was very real. There are two types of fear—fear rooted in respect, like the fear I have each time I run up a mountain, and fear that paralyzes. Anything can go wrong while I'm running in the mountains and out of fear, I prepare and I bring all the gear needed to keep me safe and warm. Healthy fear is necessary in life. But the fear that paralyzes keeps us from living in all the ways that make us unique. This is where confusion set in for me, beginning back in 1983, trying to understand the difference between the fear that was keeping me safe and the fear that was stealing my life.

I have empathy for those who live in fear, but I know the overwhelming power of choosing strength over fear. Maybe, you *also* had a monster in your life who made you feel scared and weak. Possibly, you convinced *yourself* that you are not strong. I deeply understand that, too.

Each day you wake, you can choose to believe what is true—*you are strong*.

I hope you choose to believe it,

I hope you choose to stand in it,

Unaltered and fully valid.

Be Still

"What you WANT and what you NEED will rarely agree.
Sometimes what you need is to walk into a place,
Where you know you're going to struggle, and be still.
The struggle taps at your senses;
It beckons you to find a solution;
It challenges you to try.
And when it's all over,
And you're wrecked from head to toe;
You'll finally understand something you could have never
understood had you stayed in your predictable, comfort bubble.
You'll learn you *can* endure discomfort.
You'll see that,
You're *not* alone in your exposed weaknesses.
You'll recognize you're stronger than you thought you were,
Maybe you'll even be mad about that one.
Because the truth is,
You were *always* strong,
Even in your struggle.
You were made for this life.
You were made to rise and fall again and again.
The gold is in your resilience to keep trying;
Not in a piece of *medal* that fades.
You are,
And always will be;
Wonderfully and uniquely strong for the very journey you're on.

-yellowrunner

SALLY MCRAE

CHAPTER 2

STRAWBERRY SHORTCAKE PAJAMAS

Early in my formative years, I fell in love with three sports—
gymnastics, soccer, and running. I was often the quickest on
the playground. Running made me smile—I loved moving fast.
My parents, noting my speed, signed me up for local races where
I usually came in first or second place. Sometimes, I walked to
the local park where I ran continuous loops along the perimeter
of the grass. I knew if I wanted to run well, I needed to practice
every day, which I understood as running until I got exhausted.

When I reflect on those initial years of running, I can recall
a distinct contrast between Dad and Mom's reactions to my
running. Dad was more serious and pointed out every detail about
my performance. He told me how I was supposed to breathe in
through my nose and out through my mouth, and his firm tone
before and during my races made me nervous. On the other hand,
Mama had a calming disposition and regularly pointed out the
good, no matter my performance. Mama loved to watch me run
and Dad loved to watch me win.

With my legs spinning beneath me and my breathing loud, I discovered that even when my face turned red and my body ached from pushing to maximum effort, I could still reach the finish line. To my surprise, I learned all the pain I felt while running quickly disappeared as soon as I finished. The best part of racing, well, at least when I was young, was receiving a shiny medal hanging from a piece of ribbon. No matter how tired I felt crossing that finish line, I couldn't wait to hold that medal. It was, by my understanding, the best way to make Dad proud of me.

Racing was my opportunity to impress and prove my worth. Weekend after weekend, I laced up my shoes, walked to the start line, and surveyed the girls I needed to beat. I had enough pride, or maybe desperation, to believe I could beat everyone—and I usually did. Before the word strategy made its way into my vocabulary, my only plan was to run as fast as I could for as long as possible. Sometimes I got a little too nervous while waiting for the race to start, and once an official paused the start of the race and approached me as I stood shaking on the line. He gently placed his hand on my shoulder, asking, "Are you okay?" Unknown to me, my back leg shook vigorously as if it had a mind of its own, and my tightly clenched fists pressed hard at my sides as if I were about to walk into a boxing ring. I *needed* to win.

I needed to win because by this time in my brief life, I was frequently in trouble at home. A horrible feeling swelled inside me every time the monster appeared. The pain in my punishments felt worse than the discomfort I felt in a race. That pain hurt from the first hit and remained for days to follow. Somehow, that lingering pain transformed from a physical feeling into a really terrible mental feeling. It's hard for a little girl to explain painful thoughts—thoughts that sometimes felt worse than the hardest hit. Pain in a race was part of winning, and I expected the ache to increase the closer I got to the finish line. I didn't view it as negative because I brought it on myself—I put myself in discomfort because I liked to win. Winning didn't make me feel ashamed.

I felt Dad's love and approval disappear when I got in trouble. How could I make him love me again? What achievement would shine my worth? I suppose winning a race holds a similar sentiment. As a lifelong athlete, I know the thrill of standing at the top of a podium. The overload of attention and positive feedback can bring a temporary feeling of self-worth, but I would be lying if I didn't admit that the reality of it is fleeting. It only takes seven days before another race and another champion takes the spot in the limelight. Your name is no longer first on the list in the news, the world moved on, new records are set, and a shinier medal is now on display.

In the sports world, it is common for pro athletes to find their identity and worth in the sport to which they have dedicated their lives, so when these athletes get injured, age, or retire, we hear about their feelings of loss and sadness. What will bring them the same sense of worth and fulfillment? Who are they apart from a sport that consumed their days and introduced them to a world flooded with fans and praise? I believe these are invaluable questions we must ask ourselves, regardless if we're a competitive athlete. Apart from our jobs, money, social status, or accomplishments, who are we? I hope you would still define yourself as valuable regardless of your achievements and possessions.

Maybe you remember yourself at age five or six, generally still an innocent, carefree time in life. For me, by age six, I worried. And to control that worry, I consciously studied Dad's patterns. I paid attention to when he left and returned from work. I listened for how he shut the front door and how hard or soft he closed the car door. If he furrowed his brows he was unhappy, and if he rested his hands on the back of his head he was relaxed. I listened to his conversations with Mama and remembered what made him laugh or what made him mad. Like a lion watching its prey, I hunted for ways to remain pleasing, and I became hyper aware of my mistakes and imperfections that infuriated him.

Pleasing my parents, especially Dad, became my focus. I didn't get it right early on. Sometimes I made errors, like when I was five years old and my chore was to hand wash and dry the dishes. Those darn wet plastic cups kept slipping from my hands and bouncing across the linoleum floor, apparently one too many times, because the monster soon appeared—agitated with me. I remember standing next to the counter as my short frame shook. The monster crouched close to my face and barked that if I dropped one more cup, he would punish me. Suddenly, the green Tupperware cup felt heavy. Mama had purchased this set of green and red plastic cups for Christmas—the red ones had a snowflake on them and the green ones had a little bird on them. I loved those cups, and we used them all year long—but now, this cup in my wet hands made me anxious and I couldn't grip it tightly enough. Frozen in place and unsure what to do next, I stared at the floor, hoping the monster would leave. Instead, he demanded I look into his icy eyes. I reluctantly peeked up at him, promptly dropping the cup. I had made another dreadful mistake.

I was keenly aware Dad treated me differently than my siblings, and on this evening, when Mama was away for a few hours, a terrible event took place. I did my best to understand what about me made the monster angry, because whatever it was, made me hate myself, too.

Light from the television screen in our dark living room illuminated my sisters' and my faces as I was whisked away before their eyes. They gasped in unison and within seconds, I was hanging upside down in my bedroom. The pressure around my ankles from the monster's large paw made me yelp, and I begged through choking tears, "Please! I'm sorry, No . . . please!"

But my cries were in vain. I was powerless to calm the rage he unleashed once the monster came out. He was out of control and hardened. He beat my entire body as I tried to avoid him, and through my wailing, he screamed back at me, "STOP YOUR CRYING, DAMMIT! SHUT UP!"

It was a cruel request and he knew it, and for my every reaction, he hit harder. My whole body burned, and my head spun from being held upside down. My thrashing grew weaker and my strength faded. I was helpless in his paws.

When he was done, he released his grip on my ankles and I fell onto the carpet. To finish me, the monster hurled a mouthful of insults at me as he left the room. Like venom, those insults stuck into my being, poisoning my innocence. My pale blue Strawberry Shortcake pajamas were the only childish thing about me. Like a bulldozer moving back and forth across a plot of land, his hate shaped itself into my beliefs.

Shamefully, I pulled my welted body into the bunk bed and closed my eyes. Beneath the covers, I traveled to a faraway place, but I jolted back to reality when I turned onto my back. The welts burned and I winced, slowly turning onto my side. I longed for Mama and hugged my pillow. It wouldn't have been bad if she was there, but she wasn't. Instead a reel forced itself into my mind, replaying the night repeatedly. I saw his eyes, gray and cold, and the images remained with me until I fell asleep.

A gentle hand pulled back my blankets in the middle of the night. I recognized the weeping—it was Mama. The entire house was dark except for the hallway light. I turned to face her, flinching as the mattress met my back.

"Oh my Sally, I'm so sorry . . . come to Mama."

I cautiously stepped toward her, fearful of the monster hearing me from his cave down the hall. Mama's hands turned my body as she examined the rage imprinted on my limbs, back, and stomach. It was too much for her to see and she pulled me to her chest, "I am so sorry I wasn't here Sally . . . are you okay? Sally?" Her tears rolled onto my head, and I silently looked up at her. I was learning. Mama couldn't protect me, my siblings couldn't protect me, no one could protect me—except me.

I needed to be a good girl and I needed to stop crying so much. Crying made the monster's hate increase. I had to quietly endure pain, and I needed to harden myself against the weakness that made everything worse.

My Strawberry Shortcake Pajamas

I wrestled with the power of Mama's love for me. I knew she cared about me more than anyone, but I was a bad girl. If I wasn't bad, I wouldn't have been beaten. At six, I believed my very existence was a bad thing. Ultimately, I believed being me was a problem. A problem I needed to change.

CHAPTER 3

BOY

When you hate yourself, you believe you're not good enough. You see yourself as less valuable than your peers and wrongly think misfortune and disappointment are your destiny. You stare in the mirror hating yourself, scrutinizing all the characteristics you've convinced yourself are ugly or polarizing. Worse yet, when facing adversity, you lean into low-self-esteem and quitting because you think you are not strong enough to overcome— you believe strength is a special trait for *other* people, not you. Sadly, this pattern of thought becomes normal and over time, a hardened part of how you live life.

It's natural to look for ways to change the parts of ourselves causing this self-hate. Surely our exterior is the biggest culprit— the part of us most seen by the world. Maybe if we change, we will accept ourselves. Perhaps alterations will change our situation, disappointment, or hopelessness. Change isn't a bad thing—it's good when rooted in love, but when rooted in anything else, it's sinking sand, unable to stand.

I'm getting right to the point here—*belief* is powerful, but like change, if it's *not* rooted in love, it won't last. We hear the statement all the time, "Believe in yourself!" But what exactly does that mean? For a person drowning in doubt and self-rejection, this statement is as good as dirt. But for a person who roots their self-belief in love, they are a powerful, unstoppable force. When I think about popular quotes and phrases flooding social media today, it's clear people gravitate toward words that will motivate them to change or set a goal. (I'm sure a few of your favorite quotes come to mind.) The world, however, will never be short on motivational quotes, nor will self-help books stop being published by the masses, and once we understand their substance is rooted in shallow ground, the motivation only lasts for a season and we move on to the next one.

Earlier, when I mentioned love, I wanted you to know that I'm referring to the unconditional kind. The love that endures all things, always perseveres, always hopes, always believes, always protects, and never fails. With a definition like that, I can affirm this is the most powerful force on the planet and the single most effective way to change your life.

There are two questions relating to my running career that people frequently ask me. In my almost ten years as a pro trail runner, these questions pop up whether I'm being interviewed, speaking on podcasts, or via the messages I receive through my social outlets.

1. How do you stay motivated? (Typically referencing training but also in life and through tough seasons.)
2. How do you keep going in a race? (Typically referencing when in discomfort or experiencing setbacks.)

Do you see how similar these two questions are? If I simplified the core of both of these inquiries it's centered in *hope*, *belief* and *moving forward*. The first word—*how* is the same word I have used when I question every changing season or difficult event of my life. *How* am I going to get through this injury? *How* do I work and still be a good mother? *How* do I juggle training and a career? *How* do I go on after this tragedy? *How* do I get to the finish line when I feel terrible? Don't you wish we were born with our individual life manuals—a hardback copy with our name written in gold letters across the front, *How to Live Sally's Life*. (Of course, you need to insert your own name there, but you get what I mean.) To date, I have yet to meet or hear of a human born with a personalized book on how to live life. Which brings me to my next point. You weren't meant to know all the *hows*, but there is a simple answer I like to give in response to these two most frequently asked questions—*belief*. How do I stay motivated? *Belief*. How do I keep going in a race when my intestines are in knots and I still have eighty miles until I see the finish line? *Belief*. How do I get up at 4:00 a.m. to train and then put in a ten-hour workday while raising a family? *Belief*. How do I rise from failure, heartache, and injury? *Belief*. How do I get myself out of bed when the world feels too heavy? *Belief*. It sounds basic, but when you plant that belief in love, it's strong and able to endure for all the days of your life.

Contrary to belief rooted in love is belief rooted in lies, fear, or hate. When was the last time you took a few minutes to consider what you believe to be true of yourself? Who or what influenced those beliefs? When overcome by hardships in life or when you're in the middle of a race and the discomfort overwhelms you, how do you talk to yourself? What do you believe about yourself? Do you understand that regardless of what you look like, your social status, education, or how you rate your abilities, you are strong and able to keep going? It all starts with belief—belief rooted in love.

When you see yourself as valued and loved, you understand you're worth fighting for and your confidence soars. You believe the goals you set for yourself are worth it because *you* are worth it. So you show up for the training, you keep going when you're tired, you push past all those self-imposed limits because you *are* worth it. A life worth living keeps going no matter the circumstance.

You were valuable the day you were born, even if you were born into hardship. No one is born a loser, but it's easy to let others make us feel that way. No one can steal your value unless you let them. That's one of the greatest troubles in life—letting people dictate who we are and how we are supposed to live. I'm talking about people whose motives are *not* rooted in love.

The belief I talked about earlier used to be foreign to me and so I empathize with those who struggle with *how* to believe in themselves. It's not uncommon for me to speak with college athletes, everyday career folk, parents, and so on who ask me, "Do you think I can do . . ." and then ask me to weigh in on their big goal. I'm always amazed at how many people want someone else to believe in them—to affirm that their goal or dream isn't too far out of reach. But I'm no different from you, and I have no power to dictate whether or not you can do something. But I will say, many people don't believe in themselves because of past pain, and whether that pain is from a dysfunctional family, a previous failure, loss, or rejection, it can creep into our minds and rob us of self-belief. I know people who have lived so much of their life with low-self esteem and a lack of self-belief that they can't pinpoint where it came from. It's normalized how they live and approach every decision in life.

At seven years old, I didn't like myself. Desperate to understand the monster's cruelty toward me, it only made sense that I needed to change something about myself. I focused on physical traits because I could only understand change as a superficial layer, like the way I changed from my pajamas and into my school clothes in the mornings. Staring at myself in the mirror, I wondered if the sight of me triggered the monster. I went to Mama in frustration and proclaimed that I was a bad girl and that my ugly body was gross and fat.

I told Mama I hated being a girl and that I would much rather be a boy. Boys were better than girls. Girls were weak and cried too much. I hated being weak. I thought being a boy might keep me safe. If I could punch like a boy and be strong like a boy, then maybe I would be more pleasing.

Dad was a boy.

Dad was strong.

No one ever hurt Dad.

Dad never cried.

Everyone tried to please Dad.

I needed to be a boy like Dad.

When I was seven, my older brother babysat my sisters and me on a Saturday afternoon. For fun, he challenged us to a game of toughness. He told us to stand shoulder to shoulder in the living room and as we did, I pridefully blurted out, "I'm the toughest! What do we have to do?" He explained he would punch us as hard as he could in the stomach, and whoever didn't cry was crowned "The Toughest." I smirked at the challenge and puffed up my chest like I saw the tough boys do. "I won't cry! Let me go first!" And seconds later, my brother's twelve-year-old fist came crashing into my belly, knocking the wind out of me and dropping me to the floor. Immediately, I stood back up and scowled into my brother's face. "That didn't hurt!" But it did hurt and I wanted to cry. I didn't want my siblings to think I was weak. I wanted to prove I was strong. So I forced myself to keep a straight face. I was proud of my tears for obeying my brain. Don't cry Sally. Don't cry.

These types of interactions were where I began learning how to control my mind. Even as a youngster, I thought it fascinating how I could harden myself against pain without others knowing, all the while, controlling the outcomes with my mind. I assumed my brother thought we all would cry, and I don't blame him for thinking that. He was much bigger than us and had seen on multiple occasions, tears streaming down our faces for far lesser reasons than a punch to the stomach. I wanted nothing more than to prove him wrong.

My sisters gasped when my brother hit me, but the surprised look on my brother's face quickly changed to a smile when I stood up. He put his arm around my shoulder and commended me for being strong. I won that challenge, which was all that mattered to me.

I was the toughest.

I was the winner.

I was approved.

I leaned into my "toughness" and the idea I could handle physical pain. I pridefully believed it made me better than my peers. For all my preteen years, when I stepped onto the soccer field, I used toughness as my super power. Unafraid of being hit by the soccer ball, I'd run full speed at my opponents and take a kicked ball to the stomach or face. I could hear the parents' reactions on the sidelines and I reveled in it. "Dang, she didn't flinch . . . well, she's a tough little girl . . . she's crazy . . ."

During a weekend game, I sprinted hard toward my opponent as she tried to kick the ball away, but her shot hit me square in the face. I glared at the innocent girl and meanly said, "Is that all you got?" It didn't take long before Coach gave me the nickname Nails for two reasons. He said, "You can nail the ball from anywhere on the field, and you are tough as nails!" I loved the special nickname. Being known as tough and fooling people to think the pain didn't bother me became important to me.

One hot Sunday after church, my family strolled around the local outdoor market. When Dad took off his shirt, I took mine off, too.

"Sally, what are you doing? Put your shirt back on!" Mom scolded.

But I didn't see the difference between my seven-year-old body and Dad's, except he had hair on his chest.

"But Daddy has his shirt off, Mama."

"Yes, but Daddy is a man, and you are a girl. Girls don't take their shirts off in public."

Dad shooed the issue away. "She's still little. Just let her, Diane."

And so I strutted up and down the aisles with my shirt in my back pocket. My short haircut was still growing-out after chopping it off earlier that year, so I felt I fit right in with Dad.

We rarely went anywhere to get our hair cut—Mom usually cut our hair, but one special day, Mom took all five of us to a cheap salon. While she was occupying herself with one of my siblings, I quietly told the stylist to make my hair the same as my brother's hair. Unsure of my request, the stylist called Mom over, "She's saying she wants the same cut as your son. Are you okay with that?"

"I'm not sure that's a good idea Sally. Your brother's hair is very short."

"I know, and his hair is cool, Mama! I want cool hair too! Please!"

Mom looked at me in the mirror and shrugged her shoulders, "Okay, well, the good thing about hair is that it grows back."

After the haircut, I had mixed feelings about my short hair. At first, I felt cool and tough, like my brother, but when a boy in my church class told me I looked like a boy, I punched him in the gut and sternly said, "I'm a girl! Don't call me a boy!"

But, sometimes, when I wanted to be a boy, I liked my short hair. I'd go find my brother and his friends on the playground because I wanted to be a part of their group. But then they'd coax me, "Hey Sally, go rage on that boy over there and we'll give you a quarter!" I wanted to impress my brother and the other fifth-grade boys, so I'd run wildly toward the innocent bystander they pointed to. Without hesitation, I'd jump on the boy and punch, kick, and scratch until my brother and his friends said to stop. Then they'd toss their quarters at me and laugh, "Dude, your sister is crazy!" I figured that was a sign of acceptance, but it only took a few minutes for me to feel terrible about it. Hurting others made me sad.

Other days, I loved being a girl and instead of playing kickball with the boys, I swung on the swings with my girlfriends and colored my fingernails with markers. I also loved wearing my blue dress with my dirty white sneakers because dresses made me feel pretty. I liked the way my dress turned into an enormous flower when I spun around—that is, until David pointed out my purple underwear and chased me up the slide. Just as I reached the top, he grabbed the edge of my dress, laughing as he flipped it up. Angry, I rushed down the slide and when I found David, I punched him in the stomach. "Don't flip up my dress!"

David's face scrunched up, and he turned and ran to the teacher before I could see his tears. A minute later, our teacher firmly called me to her side, "Sally, is this true? Did you punch David in the stomach?"

She peered down at me through her eyeglasses and I stammered, "Well, he lifted my dress to see my underwear!"

Aware that I could get in trouble at home, I pushed out fake tears to invoke compassion and protested, "I don't like him doing that to me!"

Thankfully, the teacher didn't take sides. Knowing we were friends, she directed us to apologize. We mumbled to each other while staring at the ground and our teacher reminded us, "Friends respect each other and I expect that from both of you."

The bell rang, and I stood still as David walked into the classroom. He avoided me for the rest of the day, which hurt because he was one of my favorite friends. Shamefully, I walked inside the classroom and sat down. I studied David's sad face from the opposite corner and dropped my head onto my crossed arms on my desk. I knew how miserable a punch felt.

Beyond my curiosity with boys versus girls, my teachers said I was an "Outstanding Citizen"—well, some of my teachers marked that on my report cards. My teachers took little notice of the days I wore a dress or if my hair was long or short, but they noted my behavior and work ethic in class. I worked extra hard to please my teachers and getting perfect scores was of utmost importance to me. Competition fueled me and if a teacher announced any type of prize, contest, or race, I wanted to win. Looking back on my records, I routinely earned school awards. Each year, I brought home paper certificates that were more or less gold to me. You name it, I probably won it: Honor Roll Student, Spelling Bee Champ, Talent Show Champ, Class President, Fitness Award, Principal's Award, Student of the Month—no matter the title, I figured out a way to earn it.

But then there were things about me I couldn't change, no matter if I was a boy or a girl—like the difficulty I had staying in my seat and being quiet in class. It was common to see my name on the board with two checkmarks next to it, meaning I got into trouble three times. I really hated those days. Year after year, my teachers hushed me and I apologized and did my best to keep my mouth closed. It was embarrassing to be reprimanded in front of my peers. To ease the situation, I stared out the window and let my imagination wander to a faraway place. Unfortunately, getting lost in daydreaming meant losing track of time and space. When I snapped back into reality, I forgot I needed to be quiet. Without fail, I opened my mouth and another check appeared next to my name.

Some days were better, like when my older sister and I were called out of class to visit with Mr. Smalley. He taught us to pronounce the letter "S," which was especially important because half the time I told people my name, I said it wrong. Sometimes kids thought I said, "Thally," instead of Sally.

I enjoyed getting out of class and walking across the schoolyard by myself. Being outside brought a sense of freedom and I craved the feeling of the sun on my skin. My favorite teachers were the ones who brought us outside to give us a different perspective. Being outside was always an adventure, and every happy feeling I experienced with my friends and siblings was spent outdoors. On the days I didn't go to the special class, I found excuses to take two or three potty breaks, delighted by every step in the sunlight.

Overall, I looked forward to going to school each day. It's where I was happiest and teachers were kind enough to point that out to Mama. "Sally is happy . . . I love Sally's bright personality in class . . ." And when Mama told me about their kind words, I thought maybe being a girl wasn't so bad. Maybe being Sally was okay, sometimes.

While my teachers persevered in their graciousness toward me, a short-tempered monster intolerant of childish behavior lurked at home.

One evening, while Mama worked in the nursery at church, Dad told us to put on our shoes because we were meeting Mama and going to Bible Study. Dad locked up the house as we hopped around the car, teasing each other with disrespectful rhymes we learned on the playground. Unknown to us, Dad heard our words and walked up behind my brother just as he blurted out another rhyme. Dad angrily interrupted, "What did you just say?"

We froze and, as expected, the monster appeared. His shoulders hunched over as he knelt toward my brother's face and then asked again, except this time, it was much louder, "WHAT. DID. YOU. SAY!"

My brother's chin quivered as he whispered the rhyme. Immediately, the monster growled, "Get back in the house— *ALL* of *YOU!*"

My sisters cried and I breathed uncontrollably. I didn't want to go in the house. Bad things happened in the house when Mama wasn't home. My hands sweat as we approached the door, and the monster quickly unlocked the handle. We paused in the entryway for a second, not knowing where to go, when he snarled, "Girls, go sit on your brother's bed. *NOW!*"

And with a swift paw, he dragged my brother to his room while the four of us ran ahead. The unknowing gnawed at us. What was he going to do? Was he going to get the belt? Why were we on the bed? The monster entered the room and we trembled as our brother was thrown to the floor. Instantly, the monster came down on top of him screaming, "You want me to break this arm!? You think it's funny to say stuff like that!?"

My brother shrieked as the monster put pressure on his arm. Desperate, I stood up and shakily begged, "No! Please … please!"

But the monster glared back at me and snarled, "SIT DOWN AND SHUT UP!"

I bolted myself to the bed, not wanting to watch, but I couldn't turn away. What's a child supposed to do in this situation? I watched, helplessly taking in every tear and grimace on my brother's precious face. My sisters and I were defenseless against the trauma tattooing into our minds, its needle full of toxic ink, repeatedly puncturing our once innocent minds with every blow. A sick feeling pushed itself from my belly and into my throat. I knew I should be on the floor, too. I said the rhyme—I *deserved* that pain, too.

The monster released the pressure from his arm and hit him all over his body. Why was he making us watch? A wave of shame came over me. My brother was taking the blame. I screamed inside, *STOP! NO, NO! PLEASE STOP!*

My brother vainly begged and apologized, but the monster's fury wasn't satisfied. It needed a few more minutes—or at least that's how I learned to measure it. Because when it got really bad, that meant it was almost over and that he was getting tired. Occasionally he went a little longer, so I taught myself to never expect the pain to end, but to always expect the pain to last longer. Oddly, this bit of control made the pain somewhat bearable and I wouldn't feel so overtaken. Measuring the monster's fury was a survival tool for me and the only way I could exist amid the chaos. Teaching myself to not be surprised by pain or its often merciless duration built a layer of endurance in me I still call upon today.

My brother and I routinely got the worst beatings in the family. I used to think it was because we were the most alike. We had similar, outgoing personalities and excelled in whatever sport or activity we tried. When I was little, I used to tell him, "We are the strong ones"—whatever that meant.

Watching the monster hurt my brother wounded me in ways I didn't understand until later in life. I saw myself in my brother that night. The one who I admired for being tough cried like I cried. He begged like I begged. He was scared and helpless, just like me.

When the monster finished, he pivoted toward my sisters and me as we cowered into each other. I gulped, fearing if I moved too much, the monster would single me out. His large body came near, and the heat from his snout made my eyes squint. I clenched my fists into my chest, attempting to make myself small. It was typical for the monster to pause after hurting us and explain the countless reasons we deserved his "disciplining." The only thing I understood from his mess of words was we were really terrible children.

The monster's voice boomed, "LET THIS BE A LESSON TO YOU!" He then commanded us to go to bed. But I didn't want to leave. I wanted to hug my brother and tell him he was going to be okay, but I was too afraid. Slowly and reluctantly, I pulled myself from the edge of the bed, unable to take my eyes off his crumpled body. I felt ashamed for not comforting him and the image of myself walking away while he lay on the floor weeping has never left me. A cloud of shame hung over me as I drifted from his room and buried myself in the darkness of my pillow.

Maybe being a boy wouldn't save me from pain.

Maybe boys are scared like girls.

Maybe boys cry and shake in fear, too.

Maybe I didn't want to be a boy anymore.

CHAPTER 4

WORK HARD. BE HARD.

In the continual pursuit of love and approval, I learned how to work. Dad was a hard worker and work consumed all of his time. If he wasn't working at the factory across the street from our house, then he was beneath the hood of our broken car trying to fix it. Any free time was spent practicing drums or coaching and refereeing soccer games. If he wasn't doing those things, then he was performing with his band at a local restaurant or bar late into the night. Dad was gone quite a bit and looking back, if he was home, the odds were against me. My only memories of spending long periods of time with Dad were when I worked with him. Consequently, I equated work with love and approval.

When I was in first grade, I began accompanying Dad to work on the weekends. I sat at an oversized, greasy desk at a battery factory with a pile of receipt books and a giant stamp imprinted with the factory's address. I liked the feeling of the stamp submerging into the ink pad, and I'd carefully align the stamp and press extra hard on the paper to get all the words to appear perfectly. Sometimes, I got tired or distracted and I'd skip pages. I wasn't always great at it, but I was learning how to follow through with a task. Dad said I could have a quarter for every book I stamped, which was a lot of money for a girl with holes in her shoes and second-hand clothes.

The factory smelled like car oil and dirt, and every inch was filthy. They brought in the batteries from the garage door openings. At the front of the factory, customers waited in a bright orange lobby while employees searched for the right battery. The building's lighting sticks out to me. I suppose light from any memory is a significant part of the vivid images and reels that replay themselves over the years. The hues and contrast, the shadows and highlights, light or lack thereof has held a powerful presence in my life. I remember being drawn to the sunlight that pushed through the large openings in the walls. Sometimes I'd stare from the desk where I was told to stay, and I'd watch the light bring out the faint red strands on my dad's head of mousy brown hair. Dad was mysterious to me. He looked like a nice person from where I sat. He smiled when he talked, and now and then, the excitement in his voice led to a burst of laughter. I didn't always understand his conversations, but I longed to understand him. I wanted Dad to smile when he spoke to me. I wanted him to be happy that he was my daddy and not mad.

One day, a gentleman walked into the factory and asked Dad if he knew how to build a fence. The gentleman owned several properties in the area and one of them needed a few repairs. Without hesitation, Dad responded with a confident, "Yes," and the man handed him his business card.

The truth, however, was Dad had never built a fence in his life, but he saw the opportunity to make money—something our family always lacked—and maybe this one job would lead to another one. I admired Dad's willingness to step into a challenge and find a solution. Nothing deterred Dad. If something in the house needed to be repaired, he learned how to fix it. If our car broke down on the side of the road, he repaired it right there on the road. And if we had a need for anything in the house, Dad could hunt it down and buy it used for cheap. Dad was relentless in finding the pathway for whatever he was after, and if he didn't find it, he created it himself. It came as no surprise that Dad drove to the home improvement store that evening and bought a book on how to build a fence. He devoured every word, and a few days later, built his first fence—and not just any fence, but a nice-looking, sturdy white fence that would undoubtedly impress the gentleman who asked him to build it. Dad's hard work excited the property owner, and he continued calling Dad offering more jobs, "Can you fix a toilet? What do you know about laying flooring? How good are you at electrical work?"

Every task was new territory for Dad, but he accepted each one, learning along the way. It didn't take long for Dad to see he could go into business for himself and so he left the Battery Factory and became a handyman—an informal title describing people who are handy in a variety of specialties like plumbing, electrical, and overall cosmetic upgrades within the home. Soon, Dad's schedule was full of jobs across the county, and he continued studying and learning new skills to make his work better.

It was fun working with Dad. I loved exploring the mostly empty houses and apartments he worked in and occasionally, we would go to homes where people still lived. Captivated by how other people lived, I stared at the pictures on their walls and the food on their counters. My great curiosity pulled me down hallways and I feigned excuses to use their bathrooms. Then, while sitting on their toilet, I imagined what it was like to live in their home. Usually, I concluded it was better than where I lived. Sometimes, Dad brought two kids to work with him, but most of the time it was just one of us who accompanied him and I volunteered as much as possible, hoping to win his favor.

When it was just Dad and me, it was my opportunity to impress him. We might have fun and laugh together. Dad had a plan for each job, so falling in line with his structure was where I thrived the most. I had a naturally strong build, and I prided myself on being able to carry his toolbox and work supplies. Dad taught me to do basic tasks, like screwing on electrical plates and ceiling fan blades. I sat on the ground with him while he laid linoleum floor tiles, and it was my job to use a hair dryer to heat the glue on each tile because Dad said it made the tile stick to the floor better. I learned how to do touch-up painting and how to keep the work area tidy. Lugging trash to the dumpster, sweeping, and vacuuming the dust from hard-to-reach corners made me feel helpful. I observed how Dad worked and asked a lot of questions. In my opinion, Dad was the smartest person I knew and his answers were often colorful and descriptive.

Working made me feel like he was proud of me. Sometimes on the weekends when we had several jobs in one day, he took me through the McDonald's drive-through and I picked out a $1.49 Happy Meal—which was a big deal because that also meant I brought home the toy from the kid's meal and showed it off to my siblings. Dad rolled down the windows as we drove, singing along to his favorite bands like Roy Oberson, Was (Not Was), and The Who. His taste in music was diverse and deep and because of him, I, too, developed a love for music. Rarely did a day go by when music wasn't playing in our home. If music wasn't playing on the radio, then Dad was probably playing with his band in the garage where he single-handedly built an entire music studio complete with sound boards, double insulation, extra shaggy carpet, and a variety of instruments, microphones, and speakers. He even learned how to build a customized drum set to accommodate his left hand. Dad's dedication to music defined most of his days and when his band came over to practice, we knew not to disturb him.

One afternoon, after a few months of working with Dad and staying out of trouble, my siblings and I played in the house while Mama shopped at the grocery store. Dad had just started band practice in the garage and firmly reminded us not to interrupt.

We bounced around the furniture, giggling, when my younger sister told me she could beat me in a foot race from one end of the room to the other. "No, you can't! I'm the fastest!"

I bantered and teased that she could never beat me and she hollered back, "Then let's race!" I skipped to the spot where the hallway and living room floors connected—one side carpet and the other linoleum. "Put your foot on the line," I said, but she laughed and ran toward the other end of the room. Mad that she started before me, I sprinted after her, determined to not let a six-year-old beat me. As I approached her, my foot caught her heel, catapulting me headfirst into the corner of our oak entertainment system. My head hit the corner with such force the sound of the collision made my sisters gasp and freeze in place, "Sally! Are you okay?"

Face down, I didn't make a sound. I silently reached for my forehead, where the pain seared and pulsated. I felt pain, but I feared the monster and sat in paralyzed silence. Thoughts of what the monster would do to me after finding out I was the reason for disrupting his band practice petrified me. At eight years old, I knew how to harden myself against physical pain—I'd rather be in pain than disrupt the monster and I believed this was how to be strong. But when I finally sat up from the ground and blood streamed down my face, my siblings screamed. I quickly bit back,

"No! Shhhh, don't tell Daddy! I'm okay, please!" I begged them to stay quiet, but one of them had already run to the garage door.

I sat like an ice sculpture on the carpet as Dad rushed toward me. An icy chill ran up my spine and I choked on my words in fear. "I'm sorry."

My siblings stood with wrecked faces, realizing they were staring at my exposed skull. I raised the hand I had used to cover my wound and numbly evaluated the blood covering it. Within minutes, I was in the car pressing ice wrapped in a rag against my bleeding head, as Dad nervously sped to the emergency room.

I remember watching the trees blur next to me as I stared out the window. I was unusually calm, and the pain clamoring around my head felt different from the pain the monster gave me. But the monster didn't join us for the car ride. As we pulled into the parking lot, relief came over me—the monster would not hurt me today.

We entered a gray, uninviting entrance of the single-story clinic and I wandered to a cold plastic chair. Dad, with notably great worry in his voice, explained the incident to a woman with brown hair. My arm was tired of holding the rag against my head, but my curiosity kept me occupied as I evaluated every object and person in the waiting room. I had been to a building like this a few times and it made me nervous. This was the place where strangers with white coats put needles in my arm. This is where people with sad faces and hunched shoulders waited for their name to be called. I stared at the back of Dad's head, hoping his face would turn toward me, and when he finally did, he looked concerned. I wasn't sure what to think, but his expression made me feel like he cared about me—maybe today wasn't such a bad day after all. The woman behind the counter stood up and peered over the ledge in my direction. Her eyes were compassionate, and she gently smiled, so I smiled back.

A moment later, Dad and I walked into a bright hallway and followed a nurse to a small room. "The doctor is coming right now, Sally, and he's going to take good care of you." She helped me climb onto the examining table and as soon as I was lying flat, a man with a long white coat and eye-glasses came through the door. His eyes were kind and his voice calmed me until he pulled out a long needle. Instantly, I squeezed my fists across my chest to hide my fear. I think I did a good job because the doctor smiled and told me I was brave. I stayed still as he put shots in my head to numb me for the sewing he was about to do. I didn't like staying still, so I stared above me and tried making shapes from the millions of dots on the ceiling. At some point in my staring, the doctor's hand appeared again, and I watched as he rhythmically poked his needle in and out of my skin, intent on closing the hole in my forehead.

The physical pain from that day doesn't stand out to me, but I'm sure I hopped off the bed with a smile on my face. I was good at smiling, even when I was a little broken. Eighteen stitches and a few decades later, the faint scar on my forehead still remains. Sometimes, I slide my finger along the hardened tissue, remembering little Sally and how she thought back then. Her ability to harden herself and minimize pain is not something I admire, but mourn.

I wish she knew it was okay to cry.

I wish she knew she mattered more than drum practice and toolboxes.

And I wish little Sally knew it was okay to feel pain and still be loved.

It was okay to feel pain and still be strong.

CHAPTER 5

DIANE

Heavenly, Divine, Bright

I love the meaning of Mama's name—*Diane*, "heavenly, divine, bright." It fits her perfectly. When I think of my childhood relationship with her, I am drawn toward the consistent, powerful feelings of being loved by her. I had a mother who truly loved me. Mama owned nothing of proper material value, but she owned a light within her that still shines today.

Diane Frances was a beautiful woman with brown wavy hair and big brown eyes, and when she laughed, she threw her head back, often making those around her laugh, too. She was born in Minnesota and grew up dancing, an art she excelled in as a teen. Her shy, introverted disposition hid from attention, but at home and around her closest friends, she was silly and fun, and she loved spending quality time with those she loved. Diane found great fulfillment in being a mother. When asked about her five children, she might have told you she wanted more—in fact, most of the minor jobs she worked involved caring for children like babysitting and working in the nursery at church. Diane never tired of caring for others.

Financial stress was a common topic in our home, but Mama was a hard worker. Constantly figuring out ways to contribute to the family income while raising five children was not a simple task, but she did it with grace. Although it never seemed to bring in enough, she chose jobs that still allowed her to be with her children. I remember Tupperware parties and Amway catalogs in our home, and when I was in grade school, she was a teacher's assistant. When I reached middle school, she enrolled in a course from home to earn her CNA certification and began working in a nursing home—a job that required applicants to be "empathetic."

Empathy was a skill that came naturally to Mama, and her ability to communicate with her children the importance of developing it was woven into some of my favorite memories with her. A few times during the holidays, while we were still little, Mama took all five of us to the local nursing home to visit with residents. Her simple words about remembering people who are forgotten have stayed with me my entire life. Nursing homes and orphanages would have remained foreign until I was an adult, had it not been for her. She explained how sometimes people live in buildings away from their families when they need extra care or when there is no one around to care for them. I remember being curious and somewhat obsessed with the idea that some people are forgotten. My youthful mind had no way of connecting to it until one Halloween night, when we all dressed up and piled into the station wagon and drove to a nursing home. Mom explained the residents had candy to give us, and we needed to use our manners and say, "Trick or Treat."

I thought it was weird going to an old brown building for trick-or-treating, but as I stepped into the stark white hallways and saw the rows of people in wheelchairs and walkers, it mesmerized me. All of them had white hair and wrinkly skin, and their faces lit up like the sun every time we came close and proclaimed in unison, "Trick or Treat!"

I watched as veiny hands moved like molasses to pick up a single Tootsie Roll and drop it into our pillowcases, one at a time. Sometimes we left the hallway and went into rooms where Mama would quietly usher us toward someone lying in bed. Initially, I didn't enjoy going into those rooms—they smelled the same as when I wet the bed at night—and sometimes the people in bed looked so sad. They wouldn't say anything at all. Mama sensed the uneasiness and gently reminded us, "Even if they say nothing to you, I promise they are happy to see you. You might be the only smile they see today." I remembered her words as we tiptoed into the next room, and walked straight up to a tiny man propped up in his bed, and with my big voice proclaimed, "Trick or Treat!" The old man's sunken face curved into a smile, and he let out a faint chuckle, "Well, hello there, young one."

I liked the feeling of making people smile, especially after learning how many of the people in the home were sick and sometimes lonely. Mama had taught us how easy it is to be kind and she said when we are kind, it makes our hearts feel good, too. When December approached, Mama took us back to the same home to sing Christmas carols. And again, we wore our smiles and sang cheerfully as we walked the halls and collected candy canes from our wrinkly, warm friends.

Mama's kindness and empathy were rooted in her unshakable faith. I have a permanent picture of her in memory, sitting cross-legged in her fuzzy robe with a big cup of steaming tea at the dining room table. Her Bible wrapped in a blue fabric cover and the journal where she wrote her thoughts and prayers accompanied her in those early mornings before the house came to life. The times I observed her in peaceful meditation kept me curious about what she was doing. Everything I knew about God, I had learned from my parents, but it was clear the way Mama talked about God differed from how other people referred to God. Sometimes, when I was in trouble, I imagined God on a giant gold chair decorated with colorful jewels. And I envisioned His face—unhappy and scowling. I wondered if, like the monster, He was waiting for me to make a mistake. But Mama gently explained that God wasn't waiting for me to be naughty and that He loved me, no matter what—even if I misbehaved. Mama said God would never stop loving me. I wanted to believe like Mama believed, but sometimes it was really hard, especially when the monster left welts on my legs before it was time to go to bed.

From time to time, after the entire house went to sleep, I crept from my bunk bed and slid beneath the curtains in my bedroom, doing my best not to wake my sleeping sisters. I liked staring at the sky and the few stars that shined the brightest against the black canvas. Curious about where God lived and trying to believe like Mama, I whispered my childish prayers to Him, "If you can hear me, can you make me fly really high? I want to fly so far away. Please God, can you make me fly?" Tears accompanied those prayers as I desperately tried to understand why my little life hurt and how I could escape it.

One morning, I wandered to the table where Mama sat and pulled up my shirt to reveal a mysterious white line across my belly. "Mama, what is this right here?"

Mama smiled and touched my stomach. "Well, it's a scar from when you were a tiny baby." Puzzled about why it was there, I continued asking questions and so Mama told me the story about my surgery when I was five weeks old. She said when I was a brand new baby, I routinely vomited up formula as soon as I swallowed it. She tried everything imaginable to get me to eat and when she was unsuccessful, inferred a bigger problem was the underlying issue. They took me to the doctor after she shared her concern. It didn't take long to diagnose me with pyloric stenosis, an uncommon condition in infants that blocks food from entering the small intestine but could be fixed with surgery. That was the only part of the story she shared with me. It wouldn't be until later in life that she shared the complete story about how I almost died from that surgery.

When I was a teen, Mama explained her anxiousness about me having surgery. The thought of my eyes closing under anesthesia while a doctor cut across my stomach frightened her. The doctor assured Mama that the procedure was uncomplicated and quick—there was nothing to be concerned about. Mama knew it had to be done, and she also knew it could have been much worse. I was an otherwise healthy baby.

When it was time for my surgery, Dad suggested he and Mom attend a church service while the surgeon performed the procedure. Horrified at the thought of leaving the building, Mama declined, but it was no use arguing with Dad. Moments later, Mama woefully stared at the hospital in the rearview mirror as they drove to church.

I don't know why Dad didn't want to stay and I don't blame him for leaving. I don't enjoy being in hospitals either, but I imagine how Mama felt as she entered that church sanctuary. I imagine her sitting in distress, watching the clock, unable to settle her mind as the thought of the tiny baby she had just birthed weeks prior was now far from her reach.

Almost two hours passed before Mom and Dad were back in the hospital. I was wheeled into the NICU to recover shortly before they arrived, which was just in time because when Mama hurriedly peered through the window and spotted me, panic set in—I wasn't breathing. The sight of my blue skin sent Mama screaming down the hallway for help—her worst nightmare had come true. They gave me the wrong dosage of drugs and I was now unresponsive. As the doctor worked speedily to revive me, I imagine Mama holding her breath, waiting for mine to return.

When I finally awoke, Mama said I let out a cry, which was a good thing because crying meant I was alive. Crying let Mama know she hadn't lost me. After hearing the full story, I affectionately accredited Mama for saving me—she was my angel.

Not only was Diane an angel, she was a wise and intuitive mother who prided herself on connecting with her children beyond hobbies and educational achievements. Mama cared about the people we were becoming. She knew, just like all mothers, that one day her children would grow up and move out of the house. As children, we didn't think about that as much as Mama did—being an adult felt like an eternity from where we stood on the playground. Children don't think about the big picture, nor do they understand the multitude of steps it takes to get from point A to point B. Children do wonderfully living in the moment, and Mama was good at living in the moment with us. Her ever-watchful eye also calculated ways to prepare us for the unavoidable difficulties the world had for us. Mama knew a thing or two about difficulties. The beginning of her journey into motherhood began with a shocking pain she had never experienced until that day she told Dad she was pregnant.

Even though Mama never climbed mountains, she has been one of my greatest sources of fuel whenever I'm running up the side of one. Because Mama lived in the moment alongside us, it allowed me to be inspired by her. I learned more from her than she will ever know.

When I first started trail running, I needed little instruction on how to run. What I needed was someone to point me to the trailhead and remind me to take the proper gear. We find the best learning in the trying, in taking the initial step and then doing it again and again. The actual act of getting up the mountain is more mental than physical. It's more mental because we have to be okay embracing the undeniable discomfort that comes with running upward.

Unfortunately, we live in a time where society teaches us to avoid discomfort at all costs. Truth is, discomfort is a vital part of the growing process. Climbing requires us to push against resistance—gravity. And when we do this continuously for miles and miles, our muscles naturally ache. Climbing makes you feel everything. My favorite thing about climbing is that it strengthens you. Resistance is the best way to strengthen your body, whether by lifting, pulling a weight, or pushing your body up an incline. The truth is, getting strong hurts. This is why Mama is my greatest inspiration when I run up a mountain. She showed me how to choose strong and keep pushing for the top, no matter the circumstance.

One of my first running races was at Whitney Park, a ten-acre park on the nicer side of town, opposite from where we lived. I still remember walking up to the start line in my black soccer shorts, faded green tank top and dirty, worn shoes. There was an intensity about my running in those early years. Some say that intensity remains today—I don't disagree. But even as an adult recalling these moments in my childhood and studying the little girl I once was, I marvel at the pure love I had for running. It hasn't changed.

Words have rarely been able to express the thoughts and feelings I've desperately tried to put on paper throughout my life, but running never misses.

When I have no words left to write, I run.

When my brain gets loud and I need a quiet space to pray, I run.

When I'm overflowing with joy and overtaken by the surrounding beauty, I run.

Running is one of the most powerful ways I communicate.

There's a home video of that race at Whitney Park—a small part of it has made its way around the internet and into a few films on YouTube. In the video, I'm standing on the start line waiting for the 1k race to start. Anxiously, I get into position, hands tightening into fists, and just as the gun goes off, my seven-year-old body reaches for a pace one would keep for a 100-meter sprint. As I make my way up the first and only climb of the race, you can hear Mama say, "If she can just get up that hill, she's gonna be okay."

Many years ago, while trudging through a tough season in my life, I replayed the home video from that race and without warning, cried. When I heard her words, it was as if a light went on in my head. I wondered if Mama knew back then that my life would continue to be filled with challenges. Was there a foreshadowing I had not seen? Maybe.

One thing is for sure, as a mama myself, I know I can say this same statement to my children, my precious Makenzie and Isaiah. I can also say this to *you*, because the truth is, we all need to know that when we hit the mountains in life and the climb feels hard that we're gonna be okay.

Sometimes it's the simplest reminders that bring us the greatest strength. And this is one of the most beautiful ways I can sum up the light Diane carried. A light overflowing with hope, strength, and rooted in love. Mama knew the strength that comes when we climb mountains and she also knew the power of hope when we keep reaching for the summit. Best of all, Mama knew her belief in me would one day help me believe in myself, too.

Mama knew a lot about strength, and this book is my chance to spread a bit of her light.

Can you hear her?

"Just get up that hill and you're gonna be okay."

Diane

CHAPTER 6

ROCK CITY

I was ten years old when we packed up our house and moved to Rock City. Located over an hour from the coast and far from friends and family, the move was bittersweet for all seven of us. I didn't know why my parents chose to move us to a city in the desert, but I understood our home in Bonita Mesa sat on a piece of land the city owned and the city planned to widen the street. In short, they wanted to tear down our little house. Even though we only rented the home, the city paid my parents a bit of money to move out because they wanted us gone quickly. That money was essential in helping my parents fulfill a dream—the dream of owning a home. Rock City was selling brand new homes for $99,000. I knew I would miss our Bonita Mesa home , but my curiosity leaned into positivity as I envisioned what sounded like an adventure in a brand new house.

When we first pulled up to our small, black and white home, I was filled with excitement! It was the prettiest house I had ever lived in. Giant mountains towered against the blue desert sky and the warm air felt like a blanket against my skin. My favorite part of the house was in the backyard. Our gray brick wall backed up to a massive, empty dirt field where sometimes the local farmers brought their sheep to graze. I spent many afternoons on that back wall, especially after a "bad day." I would stare at the mountains and landscape stretching around me. The wall was my quiet place to think and talk to God. Mama told me God heard every word I prayed—even if I didn't say them audibly—which made me feel better, because sometimes I prayed terrible things and I didn't want anyone to hear me. In the distance, on top of one hill, was a giant electrical tower that looked like a man stepping up the hill. For years, I imagined the "electrical man" going on an adventure and envisioned the places his metal feet would carry him. In my mind, he was free. And I wanted to be free—far away on the foothills, heading toward mountains or anywhere I dreamed of going. I wish I could be like the electrical man.

I still wet the bed when I was in fifth grade. It was an embarrassing secret that caused me shame because there was nothing I could do to control it. It was normal for the little kids who were potty-training to wet the bed, but not big kids like me who were planning to go to middle school the following year. To make matters worse, I grew unusually afraid of the dark. I woke in the middle of the night and lay in my urine, petrified by what I couldn't see and anxious about how I was going to change the sheets with no one knowing. Time and again, I lay there for ten minutes trying to garner enough courage to pull back the covers. Once I did, it took another few minutes to figure out a way to move without waking my sister in the bed beneath me. Our cheap metal bunk bed squeaked and shifted with the slightest movement and climbing down the ladder without making noise was next to impossible.

One early morning before the family was awake, I snuck into the garage to put my soiled sheets in the wash. I was almost successful until once when Mom opened the door to my startled face.

"What are you doing up this early?" Her concerned look made me nervous.

I made up a story in my mind, but stopped myself from blurting it out and instead admitted, "I wet the bed and didn't want anyone to know."

I stared at the ground in shame and Mom stepped toward me, "Aww Sally, are you okay?" She pulled me close and wrapped her arms around me. I rested my head on her chest and bit my cheeks, pushing hard against the tears that wanted to pour out whenever she hugged me.

"I'm okay, I just hate it." I pulled from her embrace and continued doing the laundry.

"I'll help you with fresh sheets. Is there anything you want to talk about? Something bothering you right now?"

"No. I'm fine." I was always fine.

Even with the transition to a new city, I was enthusiastic about the first day of school, which was still my favorite place to be. The fifth graders were the oldest class on campus, which made it the coolest grade, and Mr. Bledsoe was the favorite teacher. When I was placed in his class, I wondered if it was a sign that I was going to have a good year. Immediately, I saw why Mr. Bledsoe was favored by the students—not only did he play his electric piano at the end of every school day, he also had a calming, reliable way about him. No matter the day of the week or month, Mr. Bledsoe greeted the class with a genuine smile. It was the first time I had a man for a teacher, and consequently, the first time in my life where I watched a man exhibit kindness day after day. Mr. Bledsoe soon became my favorite teacher, and even today, I consider him one of the most impactful teachers I've ever had. (Mr. Bledsoe, if you one day read this book, thank you. Your kindness meant more to me than you will ever understand.)

I thrived that year as an honor roll student, a member of student council, and I performed in the talent show with my best friends. I also started helping in the preschool class at our new church and discovered a newfound love for taking care of children.

My parents signed me up for the local recreational soccer team. It was my sixth year playing and I couldn't wait for the first day of practice. Although my first couple years of soccer involved a lot of cartwheels on the goal line, I took it seriously because of my brother. My brother was a standout soccer player, and when he was twelve, his team was good enough to go to Hawaii for a special tournament. I helped my brother raise money for the trip. For months, we drove to the nice neighborhoods and we'd hop from the car with boxes of Harry & David candy bars. Selling candy door to door was exciting, especially since I got to peek inside the big houses every time someone opened the door.

After selling every box, my dad and brother packed their bags and flew to Hawaii. The experience made me believe if I worked hard on my soccer skills, then maybe I could fly on a plane, too.

When I arrived to meet my soccer team on the first day of practice, I noticed I was one of only a few girls. Not enough girls signed up, so I was put on the boys' teams. I didn't mind because most of the boys were my friends from school, and when it came time to train, I was one of the fastest on the team. By the end of the season, the coaches selected me to be on the All-Star team. I was the only girl of the fourteen players and I proudly wore my All-Star jersey, knowing I was disproving my original belief that girls were weak. I further solidified my confidence during one of our All-Star matches. After I beat a boy to the ball for the second time, his dad screamed, "C'mon Joey, you're letting a girl beat you!"

Yep, a GIRL, I smiled to myself, and minutes later I slide-tackled his son and confidently stood back up. Joey's dad didn't like that, and I smirked as I jogged down the sideline. I was strong, and I felt proud competing with the boys on the field. However, I felt bad for taking Joey down—I would have much rather slide-tackled his dad.

Whenever a new boy moved into the neighborhood, the boys would knock on my front door and say, "You gotta race the new kid, Sally. See who's fastest!"

So I'd ride my rusty one-dollar bike (purchased from the junk truck) to the park around the corner where the boys were waiting. We gathered around a make-shift start line anticipating who would win, and I bantered and teased that I couldn't be beat. I don't remember losing, and the boy who lost was teased—it was a double-edged sword. I'd win with a smile, waving my hands in the air, proclaiming no boy in school could catch me, while the boy who lost hung his head in embarrassment. Sometimes I felt bad and chimed in, "Well, I beat all the boys here, so don't feel bad." Then we played football until the sun went down and I rode back home with grass stains on my jeans and dirt beneath my fingernails.

Even as I got older, I still preferred playing with the boys—not because I wanted to be one anymore, but because it was more fun. I was friends with girls, but many of the girls I knew still wanted to do things that were boring compared to ball sports and riding bikes in the dirt. Most of my girlfriends wanted to play with dolls or paint their fingernails, which I did occasionally, but there was another hidden reason I preferred playing with the boys over the girls. Most of my girlfriends owned more than I did, or so it seemed. I noticed with great detail all the nice things they had in their rooms—closets full with the latest fashion trends, several options for shoes, jewelry, nail polish, and cute pajamas.

I marveled at what my friends had and went home complaining about what I didn't have. It wasn't until we moved to Rock City that I paid attention to material possessions. I was always content with what I had, until I started comparing.

When we lived in Bonita Mesa, I was surrounded by kids who seemingly had the same stuff as me. At Abundant Elementary School, most of the students qualified for free lunch and it was normal to wear the same outfit every third day. Some of my best friends, like Socorro and Aurelio, came from big families and like me, shared a bedroom with several siblings. We bought our clothes from thrift stores and clearance racks. *Most* days our bodies were clean, but when there are lots of people in your family, it's better to take a shower every other day.

But Susie, my new friend in Rock City, lived six houses down from me. Susie and her sister had their own bedrooms, and I loved how Susie's room looked just like a picture in a magazine. Susie had everything I wanted, and it seemed she had new clothes every week! Her hair was always styled just right, and I never understood how her nails always looked nice. One time Susie tried to show me how to file my nails, but I couldn't get them to look like hers—which after a while was okay, because doing nails was boring. Susie didn't play in the dirt like I did, so her hands were always clean. I'm sure she took a shower every day because she smelled like flowers, and when we got to middle school, she got braces on her teeth—which Mama explained cost more than both of our cars put together. Maybe that's why I enjoyed playing with the boys. When I was with the boys, I didn't feel bad about myself. The boys I knew had little interest in what I owned or how many times I wore the same pair of dirty shoes. The statement, *Comparison is the thief of joy*, is true. And upon reflection, Susie did nothing to make me feel bad. I blame the jaded yet actual idea that more stuff meant a person was more valuable. Much of how I felt was what I *chose* to believe in my head.

One of my favorite friends and secret crush was Ryan, who lived a couple of doors down in a blue two-story house. Ryan and I were both in fifth grade and we played on the same soccer team—except I was faster and had better footwork. Ryan's mom, Cathy, became good friends with my mom and sometimes when Mama visited with Cathy, I'd wander up to Ryan's room. Ryan didn't try to impress me with his stuff or a tidy room when I went over, which made me think he didn't care that I wasn't always tidy and well put-together. There were clothes on his floor and lots of baseball gear. Ryan was one of the best baseball players in the city and I loved that he liked talking about sports because any type of sporting event excited me. I enjoyed hanging out with Ryan more than Susie, and even though I had horrible hand-eye coordination, I wanted to throw the baseball with Ryan. One morning, after arriving at the bus stop together, I told Ryan, "Throw me your best pitch! I bet I could catch it!"

Ryan laughed at first, knowing well that I couldn't catch if my life depended on it. "Do you know how fast I can throw, Sally?"

His response, of course, only made my pride come out in full force, "Yes! And I bet I could catch your fastest pitch!"

My proclamation caught the attention of our friends standing nearby and they laughed and teased me, "Sally, Ryan is literally *the best* pitcher! There's no way you can catch one of his pitches!"

I continued coaxing Ryan, who shrugged his shoulders and said, "Fine, I'll pitch to you—but you're gonna need this." He handed me his mitt. I smiled, and having never put a mitt on in my life, slipped it on the wrong hand. Ryan giggled, "Let me show you. Are you positive you want to do this?"

I responded, "What are you afraid of?"

Ryan laughed and shook his head as he walked away, "Okaaay, Sally."

I didn't know the first thing about catching a baseball in a mitt, but I figured it couldn't be all that hard. Just stick your mitt up and catch the ball as you see it coming toward you, *easy*. Ryan was now standing by the group of kids who taunted me and I stood alone, a mere thirty feet away. All I remember about what happened next is hearing myself say, "Go ahead Ryan, show us how fast you can throw!"

The next thing I remember is Ryan's horrified face peering into mine, "Sally? Holy crap are you okay? Did you know you put the mitt in front of your face?" I stared at Ryan in a trance, confused how I went from standing to lying on the sidewalk. An intense pain poked around my upper lip, but I didn't want Ryan to think I was a wimp, so I dizzily grabbed his hand as he helped me stand.

"Why are you looking at me like that?"

The words came sloppily out of my bloody mouth as Ryan half smiled, "Your lip is huge. I hit you square in the face."

I gently touched my swollen mouth and asked, "Am I bleeding?"

Ryan's expression made me worry as he answered, "Yes! Let me see your lip—there's blood on your face." I turned my upper lip to reveal that the backside was split open. At eleven years old, we didn't know what to do, and I didn't want to walk back home and tell my parents what happened. A few minutes later, the school bus arrived and as we settled into our seats, I remembered it was spring picture day at school! I glanced at Ryan next to me, who was now pale white. His voice sounded worried, "I'm so sorry, Sally."

Ryan was one of my kindest friends and I saw how bad he felt. I also considered that maybe he thought he would get in trouble, so I smiled into his face, "It's okay! It was my fault! Don't be sorry. My school picture is going to be hilarious!" We both laughed and when we arrived at school, I casually went to the nurse's office for an ice pack. I probably needed stitches, but it eventually healed just fine—well, except for the hairline crack on my front tooth. I still have that, and whenever the light hits just right and I catch a glimpse of it, I remember Ryan.

Later in the school year, the boys and girls started talking about who they liked. My friend Beau told me he liked me, and then Jose said he liked me, too. I never told Ryan I liked him, but I told Vincent he was cute. Joseph said he had a crush on me, and Brian wrote me long notes. On Valentine's Day, the boys put extra candy with mushy cards in my Valentine's box and sometimes they drew pictures for me or sat next to me at lunch.

There were a lot of changes happening in fifth grade and I was starting to grow up. I learned moving to a new place like Rock City wasn't that bad, and even when transition felt hard, after a while, I adjusted and the awkward parts about meeting new people eventually wore off. It didn't take long to understand kids around me were also learning about friendships and fitting in. Everywhere I went, I found a way to make friends—at school, on my soccer team, at church, and around our neighborhood.

But I wondered if there were kids like me on the inside. Kids who struggled with shame. I doubted the other kids wet the bed and feared the dark. Maybe no one came from a home like mine—and there was no way I was going to ask the questions needed in order to find out. I didn't need people to know those parts of me. I wondered if I really fit in because even with all those friends, sometimes I felt *extra* lonely.

CHAPTER 7

GYMNASTICS

I grew up in the era when American gymnastics was exploding with superstars like Kim Zmeskal, Kerri Strug, and Shannon Miller. Completely lacking the knowledge of what it took to excel in this sport of perfectionism and gravity defying acts of strength and power, I wanted to be an Olympic gymnast. I suspect that was due to my wild imagination (which has hardly dwindled over the years) mixed with my stubborn belief that if I just worked hard enough, I could do any and everything I dreamed.

I was a late bloomer with a petite frame until I was sixteen years old. At age twelve, I weighed a mere eighty-three pounds (thirty-seven kilograms) and stood only four foot, six inches tall (137 centimeters). In my mind, I had the ideal build for a gymnast. The only problem was we didn't have extra money to pay for the expensive classes that come with "real" gymnastics lessons. When I was five, Mama enrolled me in the city class at the local gymnasium. For the first couple years, Mama took my older sister and me to the gym twice a week. While she sat in the squeaky wooden bleachers, we rolled around on thin blue mats beneath basketball hoops. In one corner, there were balance beams, and in the other two corners, a vault and a set of bars. I loved doing backflips, but I especially liked the balance beam. When we were nine and ten years old, and after my sister and I advanced through the skills, Mama got a call from Coach Anja. "Your daughters are doing wonderfully in the lessons, and I believe they are ready to skip two levels."

Mama delivered the news as my sister and I bounced around the living room, doing cartwheels and handstands as if to confirm our advancement. We had recently learned to do aerials and back tucks, and enthusiastically talked about the possible new skills we would learn. But not long after the advanced class began, we moved to Rock City, where I focused more on soccer. I still thought about gymnastics and frequently missed the joy I found flipping across the mats or balancing on the beam. One day in the middle of my seventh grade year, I told Mama I wanted to take lessons again. Pointing to the posters of my favorite gymnasts hanging on my bedroom walls, I told Mama about my very serious plans to "get super good at gymnastics" and then go to the Olympics. Mama knew the unlikelihood of my Olympic dreams coming true, yet she graciously entertained the thought with me and said, "I think you can do anything, Sally."

Hopeful, I pushed her on the subject and said, "I want to go to a real gymnastics class. You know, a place that has springs in the floor and foam pits, not like the one in Costa Mesa on the basketball court."

A few days later, after doing some research, Mama told me the price of gymnastics was $160 a month and then gently explained that we could not afford it. I bitterly asked, "Why do the rich kids get to do everything? It's not fair!"

Mama wasn't impressed with my response, and firmly reminded me of the many things I had, including the chance to play soccer and live in a nice house. I apologized, but complained again, "Do you think we will have more money later?"

Mama knew gymnastics meant a lot to me, and instead of lecturing me on the realities of life and the financial stress of having five kids, she challenged me to make my own money. By this time, at twelve years old, a few families in the neighborhood had asked my older sister and me to babysit, so I took Mama up on the challenge and asked her for help in securing more babysitting jobs.

After brainstorming, Mama suggested I make paper signs and hang them on the mailboxes in the neighborhood. She said, "Every time the mail is checked, someone will see your sign." Her idea worked and after a few days, I picked up a couple jobs. Mama also suggested doing something extra while babysitting, like cleaning the kitchen or vacuuming. I thought her idea was brilliant and anytime a new family hired me, I told myself I was going to be the best babysitter they ever had. I played games with the kids and prepared dinner. Then, after putting the children to bed for the night (which I quickly learned was the most chaotic hour of babysitting) I would clean the entire house. If there were clothes in the dryer, I folded them and left them on the couch. I washed and dried the dishes, vacuumed, swept the floors, and tidied up the way Mama had taught me. Apparently, moms liked it when I cleaned the house, and I began getting babysitting requests three and four times a week. After a few months, I had enough money to enroll myself in *real* gymnastics lessons.

On a Tuesday evening, Mama and I made the twenty-minute drive down the freeway to the gymnastics center that had once, only been a dream in my mind.

"Oh Mama! It's amazing here! Look at all the balance beams! They have two trampolines and four sets of bars . . ." I continued pointing out the details with such excitement, I didn't hear the coach walk up.

"Hello, are you Sally?"

I popped up, "Yes, that's me!"

"It's wonderful to meet both of you in person. I talked to your mom on the phone, and she told me you have several years of experience doing gymnastics?"

I grinned and stated, "Yes, and I want to compete!"

The coach smiled, "That's great to hear. I want to do a quick assessment with you. Can you show me a handstand pirouette?"

I looked to Mom for directions. The coach sensed my hesitation and said, "Let's start with a handstand. Can you hold a handstand for ten seconds?" I smiled and shot up into a handstand, paying attention to every cue—tuck the hips, straight arms, toes pointed, legs together, chin to chest, eyes forward. "Beautiful handstand, Sally. How about a back-walkover . . . splits . . ." She continued calling out each move and when I was unsure, I'd give a side glance to Mama and she'd grin and nod with the confidence she desperately wanted me to have.

Once the assessment was over, the coach told us to wait while she chatted over the results with another coach. Fumbling with my hands next to Mom, she commented, "You did great, Sally. I could tell you were trying your best."

I leaned into her and said, "But I messed up a lot, too. What if I'm not good enough to be here?"

Mama put her arm around me and hugged me to her side, "Let's see what they say. You're always so hard on yourself."

A few minutes later, the coach delivered the news, "Sally, we have a spot for you on the developmental team. I think you have a lot of potential and we want to work with you on some key skills before putting you on the competition team. How does that sound?"

I smiled with a big, "Yes!" And even though I didn't know what "developmental team" meant, I was overjoyed to hear there was a spot for me.

The coach asked, "Do you want to meet your teammates?"

I jumped from my chair. "Yes! Will I do a class today?"

Smiling at my excitement, she responded, "Well, they've just finished training, but tomorrow night is the next session. The girls are stretching right now. How about I introduce you?"

I dreamed of this moment for years—a *real* gymnastics facility where I could finally compete. My imagination soared as we followed the coach, trying to guess which group of girls I would be joining. One group was performing on the floor and I watched as they powered their bodies through the air with ease. I whispered to Mama, "Those girls look like they're eight years old and they're already doing flips like that!" When we got to the balance beams, I again watched in wonder as girls much younger than me performed tricks I couldn't even do on the floor.

Now approaching the mat area, I saw a group of girls stretching, and then my heart started racing. *Please don't tell me this is my group, please, no.*

But then the coach perked up, "Girls, I want you to meet Sally. She is your newest teammate as of today, and I wanted to introduce her to you before your next session tomorrow night." I stood next to the coach and smiled, despite what I was feeling inside.

One girl blurted out, "How old are you? You are big!" It was the first time in my life someone called me "big," and a sour feeling swirled in my stomach as I responded to her. "I'm twelve."

Then came a clamor of voices.

"How come you are on our team?"

"You are the biggest girl!"

"Why aren't you with the big kids?"

The coach interjected, "All right girls, that's a lot of questions for Sally. This is her first time attempting competitive gymnastics, and we are thrilled she is here with us." I smiled nervously, realizing many of the girls were similar in age to the kids I was babysitting. I felt out of place. It made sense to be bigger than kids four and five years younger than me, but I concluded my size and age had something to do with my capability.

Until this point, my petite frame was something people often pointed out. I was usually the smallest kid in the class and it was becoming more frequent that kids would tease and try to pick me up, as if I was a toy stuffed animal. And even though I was in middle school, I still shopped in the little kid section in the clothing stores. I'm pretty sure I wore size 6x for four years straight. But how was I suddenly "big?" How did I not fit into this sport? Was I too late to be a good gymnast? Should I have started lessons at three years old like many of these girls had? We could have never afforded that! Was I missing out on doing something I loved because of money? It seemed most of the kids who were my size or who looked similar in age were in advanced classes, and the younger, smaller kids were in the beginner classes. Letting my insecurity think the worst of the situation, I felt dumb standing there.

The coach continued, "Sally, tell the girls where you go to school? Maybe some of them go to the same school as you." I looked around the group. Only one of the ten girls looked similar in age as me, "I go to Wildflower Middle School and I'm in seventh grade."

And again they responded, "I'm in second grade!"

"I'm in fourth grade!"

"Is that a big kids' school?"

The coach clapped her hands, "All right girls, session is over. Let's help clean up the gym." All at once, the girls popped up and scattered in every direction. I watched in wonder as they hustled like ants to carry mats, spotting pads, and blocks back to their designated places.

My eyes were drawn by one girl flipping across the floor, muscles poking out from every inch of her body—she couldn't have been a day over eight years old. The coach noticed me watching and said, "That's Anna, she's on the Level 9 team."

Still staring in amazement, I asked, "How old is she?"

The coach casually responded, "She's eight. Isn't she fun to watch?"

I agreed. Watching her flip across the floor was incredible to witness. It shocked me that someone so young could possess such power and control. "She's amazing. I bet she will go to the Olympics."

The coach smiled, "Yes, she says that's her dream."

I stood for a moment more and then trudged back to Mom and mumbled, "I'm ready to go."

Staring into the black sky as we drove down the freeway, Mama sensed something on my mind. She broke the silence and asked, "So, are you excited? That was pretty cool, huh?"

Her cheery voice didn't change my mood. I was upset and blurted out the heaviest thing on my mind, "I'm the oldest on the team! That was so embarrassing!"

Mama tried to encourage, "Sally, I bet not a single kid in that gym worked as hard as you did to get there. I know I don't tell you enough, but I'm proud of you for working all these months to save money. I hope you can be proud of that."

She tried to comfort me, but I couldn't see the good in the situation, so I pushed her away, "What does it matter! I worked hard and now I look like a dork! Did you see all the *little* kids on my team? How did I *actually* believe I was any good?" My face burned with embarrassment and my mind wandered to the idea that the other kids felt the same way about me.

Mama reached for my hand and squeezed it, "Tomorrow will be different and who knows, you might love it."

The next night, we drove back to the gym and although I was self-conscious, Mama encouraged me to not worry about my skills but focus on getting to know my teammates. "Enjoy yourself Sally. There are a lot of girls who dream of the opportunity you have! Go have fun!" I thought of her words as I joined my team on the floor. By the end of the session, although I hadn't mastered any new skills, I learned all my teammates' names.

Two months after my first training session on the developmental team, and just as Mama predicted, I grew to love it. After accepting I was the oldest, I understood because of my age, the younger kids looked up to me. Each week we spent three evenings learning new skills, perfecting the basics, and giggling like sisters.

With every session, I humbly discovered I wasn't as skilled a gymnast as I imagined in my head, a lesson I needed to learn for myself. I wondered if Mama already knew that? She told me she believed in me and encouraged me to work hard, but I don't recall her saying I was "unrealistic." Maybe Mama knew I'd learn the truth on my own. Perhaps that's why this story holds power in my life. Mama helped me focus on the work and not the outcome.

There's nothing wrong with dreaming big and aiming high. Any dream worth working for will typically feel *too big, too scary, or unrealistic*. I say, go for it anyway! Whether or not we achieve the goal, we'll be far closer than if we never tried at all. Often, it's the lessons we learn that become more valuable than the *actual* goal. I think Mama was wise—pointing me toward a journey that demanded I commit and show up—regardless if I was skilled. If I wanted to be the best at anything in life, this experience taught me it was going to take a lot more than just stubborn determination and a positive mindset. Being the best took disciplined, consistent training day after day, year after year, regardless of my age or size (this lesson will stay with me for the rest of my life).

At twelve years old, I was working hard and learning how to build relationships with my babysitting clients. Anytime I put money in my wallet, I was proud of myself. Paying for my gymnastics classes made me appreciate the lessons a little more. When I took an honest look at my skill level, it pushed me to take what I learned in class and put in the extra practice at home. I was never the most skilled or a standout on the team, but I do believe, I worked the hardest.

One Saturday, Coach announced a group of us would move to Level 5. Excited, I asked if I was part of the group moving up and she replied with a happy, "Yes, Sally!" Elated by the news, I glanced at Mama sitting nearby. Her smile matched mine. It took me three months to master key skills in each event and now I finally got to slip into my first official competitive leotard.

The parents walked toward our team as Coach continued with important announcements.

"Two weeks from today, we begin mandatory dance classes. This is necessary for all competing gymnasts. Dance classes cost an additional sixty dollars a month, so you can expect to make the payment in two weeks."

My heart sank. I already felt stretched by the $160 a month. I looked at Mom and she gave me her *oh shoot* smile. Defeated, I stared down at my feet, knowing I was the only girl on the team overwhelmed by the additional cost.

For the next two weeks, I wrestled with the extra fee. It required me to get more babysitting jobs, which felt overwhelming because I was already working three days a week in addition to gymnastics, school, and soccer. I stressed over the decision but concluded gymnastics was too expensive.

After taking my last class and saying goodbye to my team, I cried myself to sleep for months. The bitterness I felt about money and how it dictated my decision made me angry. But it didn't stop there, I struggled with relinquishing the joy I had found in gymnastics. Why had I worked so hard for something that in the end, only broke my heart?

Months later, the school announced sign-ups for the upcoming talent show. On the drive home from school, I talked with Mom about performing. "I could put a gymnastics routine together."

Mom encouraged me, "Go for it!"

For the next few weeks, I practiced in the living room, scribbling down each step of my routine on a piece of notebook paper. I sorted through music and chose an instrumental track from Disney's Beauty and the Beast. Mama was my audience, and every night I ran down the hallway and flipped across the living room. She applauded, giving me the confidence to go through with the performance.

The day of the talent show arrived, and I packed my black and neon pink outfit-I felt confident every time I slipped into it.

When it was time to perform, a thin blue tumbling mat was set at the center of The Quad just like the ones I used in my first lessons as a gymnast back on the basketball court in Bonita Mesa. Everyone in the school was seated on all four sides. A wave of nerves rushed over me as I stepped onto the edge of the mat and bent backward, hovering just above the ground. My heart raced, waiting for the first note to play. When it started, a rush of adrenaline took over. I twirled to a standing position and flipped down the straightaway. This was my first and last time performing a gymnastics routine in front of a crowd. Soaking in the moment, I concentrated on every music note and movement with a huge smile. For a short one minute and twenty seconds,

I was a world class gymnast—a fearless competitor, capable of nailing every tumbling pass. Executing each part just as I had practiced it, the routine was over just as soon as it started. The music ended right as I finished the final tumbling pass, and I gracefully paused into my final pose. With my arms across my chest and my torso tall, the audience erupted into cheers.

An hour later, I was awarded first place and a check for fifty dollars. Winning that prize was and still is, one of my favorite life achievements.

Our work is not in vain when we give our best. Too often, the dreams we have for ourselves are smaller than what awaits us down the road. My life's story was never meant to tell the journey of becoming an Olympic gymnast, although at the time, I couldn't think of anything more grand. The most valuable part of my season in gymnastics had more to do with learning to commit to a goal than how well I stuck a dismount from the bars. I learned to put my hand on the plow and do the work day after day, regardless of the result. I was preparing for my future.

CHAPTER 8

THE BALANCE BEAM

Conditional love is the worst kind of love. When I think about why people stay in abusive relationships, I think of the tangled struggle between the hot and cold moments. Often, victims are caught in a balancing act of extremes between a bout of intense pain and conditional love. It's easy to trust abusers when they pull you along for months doing nothing to harm you, and then—without warning—they strike. They use conditional love to make you stay while reminding you of all the good they did for you in the past, and then they gently tell you the pain you are feeling is sincerely caused by no one except *you*. And as the months and years pass, you believe in conditional love. You believe you are not worthy of *real* love, the kind that loves you no matter what. They make you believe you are a lesser being, and the longer you stay, the weaker you become—and the more you succumb to the shitty, conditional love.

I do my best to remember the good days of my childhood, the happy memories, and the laughter, but mostly, those moments are tied to my mom and siblings.

Despite his harshness, I still longed for Dad's approval, for him to be proud of me, to tell me that despite my flaws, he loved me. I wanted to look into his eyes and see love. I wanted to look into his eyes and not be afraid.

There were good moments with Dad, glimmers of joy that I wished I could plant into the soil, hoping they would grow. Moments that made me feel like he loved me, but sometimes those moments also confused me. For as quickly as he put a smile on my face, he took it away, reminding me of my many imperfections, making me believe I was nothing but a disappointment.

One good memory always sticks out in my mind. When I was in eighth grade, Dad built me a balance beam. He put carpet around a wooden 2x4 and laid it in the grass in our backyard. It was the nicest thing he had ever done for me—I felt known and seen. I spent hours practicing the routines I learned with my gymnastics team. Every day I stepped onto the beam, it reminded me of who made it for me—no one had ever made something so grand just for me.

The balance beam, in my humble opinion, is the toughest apparatus in gymnastics. Already a perfectionist sport, the balance beam demands every movement and every pointed toe to be perfect. There is literally no room for mistakes, as the balance beam is a mere four inches wide. A slight misstep, and you will fall. Additionally, the beam stands 4.1 feet above the ground. When you're on the beam, you're on display for all to see, to see your every move—perfect or flawed.

The relationship I had with Dad was like living on a balance beam. I needed to execute each day perfectly. In the beginning, I fell off the beam a lot, but only because I was learning about the parameters in which I needed to stay. It took a few beatings and a handful of cutting words before I understood the narrow space in which I could exist, so I learned to be perfect. I mastered the art of standing on one foot. And I always focused my eyes forward, carefully planning my next move. I learned to become comfortable being on display and to smile and to appear pleasing. I was well rehearsed, focused, and all together . . . *desperate*.

The same year Dad made the balance beam, I continued building my resume of impressive achievements. I was the eighth grade class president, an honor roll student, and held one of the lead roles in the school play. Staying out of trouble was on top of my list each day, so I helped around the house, mowed the lawn, continued babysitting and saving money, and volunteered at church. I tried my best to be perfectly pleasing.

On the day of my eighth grade graduation, I stood in the parking lot with Mama, hands sweating, anxiously scanning through notecards. As the class president, I was asked to give the graduation speech and it was an honor I looked forward to all year. I told Mama how nervous I was and she reassured me (for the hundredth time) my speech was going to be great. But, deep inside, I doubted myself. I wanted my speech to be perfect. I already knew Mama was proud of me, but I wanted Dad to be proud of me, too.

I sat in the front row and when it came time to approach the microphone, I took a deep breath and looked into the sea of faces. With a big smile, I relaxed, fully focused on executing each word perfectly. When I finished, the applause brought a smile to my face, and I walked happily back to my seat.

I couldn't wait for the ceremony to end, to run to my parents and hear what they had to say. Mama embraced me first and with a big smile told me she was proud and hugged me tightly. I squeezed her back and said, "Thank you for helping me!"

I then turned to Dad, eager to hear his thoughts and more than ready for what I thought would be words of approval. But instead, he stood there gripping his camera, and to my horror, the monster appeared. His icy eyes glared at me, and then he bent down and snarled into my ear, "You are so stuck up, Sally! You should have seen how your classmates were reacting to your speech. They were *disgusted!* You have no friends! Everyone thinks you're selfish!"

I froze as his hate oozed into my ear. The surrounding crowds blurred and moved slowly as my heart hardened against the tears fighting to push from my eyes.

He wasn't proud of me.

He was disgusted with me.

And I believed *every* word.

I was ashamed.

He then took a step back, and without missing a beat, Dad appeared and directed me, "Okay, Sally, let's get a picture of you in your graduation dress."

And just as I trained myself to do again and again, I got back on the beam, tall torso, big smile—snap, snap—picture perfect.

My heart races every time I watch a balance beam routine. Those who have graced the apparatus understand the demands of executing a flawless performance. Sometimes, after a gymnast finishes her routine, I try to imagine what's going through her mind. Is she recounting the things she did wrong? Is she proud of herself? Does she know the depth of her strength? Does she know that even when she falls in front of thousands, she's still wonderful?

Have you ever seen a gymnast embrace her coach after a *flawed* performance? My eyes are watering, envisioning the times I've observed those first few seconds when she descends the steps and buries her head into her coach. I used to cry as I watched on TV from my sofa, questioning why it brought tears to my eyes.

But the older I got, I knew why.

Because to be loved when we are flawless is expected.

But to be loved despite our flaws is the greatest love of all.

It's the love we all long for.

the balance beam

"You don't have to stand on the beam my friend.
But if you do,
just be *you*.
And when you fall,
you're still great;
still *loved*;
flawed and all."

-yellowrunner

CHAPTER 9

COSTUMES

"She said I was too small!" I sat on the kitchen counter wearing yellow soccer shorts and my favorite vintage, yellow, happy face t-shirt. But I wasn't happy. I was offended and discouraged, and I waited for Mama to take sides with me. Mama was used to listening to me chatter about my day. My descriptive stories helped her understand what made my day great, okay, or terrible. Today was "terrible" because my teammate told me I was too small to be a competitive soccer player.

Not long after my gymnastics dreams were crushed, I decided to take soccer more seriously, and I believed I had a better chance at succeeding in soccer than any other sport I was doing at the time. Lucky for me, women's soccer was gaining popularity in the 1990s and more opportunities were appearing for women to make a career in the sport. As I started my first year in high school, I contemplated all the ways I could get into a four-year college. No one in my family had a college degree, and I wanted to be the first. College was my ticket to freedom and the only way I could afford to live away from home. A scholarship meant far more to me than I ever shared with my peers. College was going to rescue me.

I watched as Mama cracked dry spaghetti in half over a pot of boiling water. With so many mouths to feed, she thought breaking the pasta in half would increase the amount of food we had. She paused to look at me and asked, "Do *you* believe you're too small?"

Already fired up, I replied, "No! But why would she say that? I mean . . . I *am* one of the smallest on the team, but I scored eighteen goals this season!"

Mama drew in a chuckle at my frustration. "You're an excellent soccer player, Sally, and I see all the extra training you do in the backyard. I'm sure your teammate wasn't trying to be mean."

I grabbed a stray piece of spaghetti, flipped it around my fingers, and continued, "Well, she also said I won't get a soccer scholarship to college because I don't play on a club team. Everyone plays on a club team except me, Mama!"

Mama nodded her head quietly. She did that a lot when I ranted and sometimes it just made me talk more, so I kept going, "I'm not going to ask why I can't be on a club team, 'cuz I already know what you're going to say! *It's too expensive.* EVERYTHING is too expensive. It's not fair! All my teammates have the nice Adidas cleats and name brand training uniforms from their club teams— and look at me! My used cleats are from the thrift store and they're white! Nobody has white cleats! The rich kids get *everything*! They get to play on club teams and wear the best gear! It's so annoying!"

Mama was now scooting ground beef around in an iron skillet. Later, she would mix the boiled spaghetti and a can of tomato sauce together with the meat. It was a common dish in our home—cheap and simple. She paused and rested her wooden spoon on the counter and then smiled into my stormy eyes. Her energy was calming as she spoke. "You're right, we can't afford club soccer. It costs over $500. But don't forget that you get to play on the varsity team at a nice high school. Also, our family gets free registration for AYSO because your dad volunteers a lot of his time in the soccer league. You get to play on *two* teams, Sally."

I scowled the same way any teenager does when a parent lectures. Mama was saying everything I didn't want to hear, and I resented her for being right. She always reminded me to be thankful for what I had, but it was hard to be grateful when it seemed everyone around me was "blessed" with more than me. *Why couldn't I have what they had?* My youthful mind could only understand that they had more than me because their lives were more valuable than mine. The opportunities of my peers to be on club teams and hire private trainers meant they had a better chance of being discovered by college scouts. Everyone knew that college scouts rarely went to the high school soccer games. Scouts cared about what club team you played for and the tournaments you played in. From my perspective, the rich kids were set up for success because they were born into money. More money, more opportunities, and I didn't think it was fair.

I responded, "Mama colleges don't care about AYSO, and some of the girls laughed at me today when they found out I still play on the AYSO recreational team. They said that's where kids play when they're not good enough for a club team!"

Mama drained the grease from the hamburger meat into an oversized coffee can she kept in the freezer. Dad said pouring grease down the kitchen sink clogged it, so she stored it in the freezer throughout the week while making dinner. I watched as the hot grease melted the top layer of cloudy frozen slime.

Now facing me, Mama asked, "Have I ever told you the costume story?"

I giggled, "No, but I'm guessing this is a Halloween story?" Mama laughed and then took me on a journey back to her high school days. "I loved dancing. It's all I wanted to do, and I was actually a talented dancer. My teachers said I could make a career in dancing if I wanted." Her eyes lit up as she continued speaking. "One day, I invited my best friend Trudy to my house. I had a big performance coming up, and I wanted to show her the costumes I planned to wear. As soon as she saw them, she burst out laughing. For days she teased me about my costumes, so I quit dancing."

Mama paused and went back to the stove and poured the tomato sauce over the cooked meat. Dumbfounded, I asked, "Wait, is that the entire story? You just quit because she made fun of your costumes? I thought you said you *loved* dancing? Why did you quit?"

Mama smiled and replied, "I wanted to fit in. I didn't want people to think I was weird or dorky because of my costumes, so I stopped dancing." Her story shocked me because it didn't seem like something Mama would do.

I sadly asked, "But why would your *best* friend do that?" I hopped off the counter and gave Mama a hug and said, "That's a sad story. Also, Trudy is the *worst* friend ever!"

Mama laughed and said, "Oh, it's okay. It happened a long time ago. But there is a reason I'm telling you this story, Sally. I don't want you to make the same mistake I did. Dance classes were *not* cheap. My family *had* the money to pay for all types of dance classes and pretty costumes. I also had talent, but all those things didn't guarantee me anything. I didn't believe in myself, and as soon as someone made fun of me, I threw it all away."

Mama spoke seriously now and I listened, studying her eyes as she went on, "Sally, I wish I had the money to put you on a club team. I would sign you up in an instant. But I don't want you to believe that being on a club team is the only way to achieve your dream. Never let anyone tell you what you can or can't do based on what you look like or because of what you have or don't have. It's about believing in yourself and working hard. Just keep working harder than everyone else. Also . . . I think you're just the right size for Sally."

She pulled me tightly to her chest and kissed me on the head. I squeezed her back and said, "You're the *best* Mama . . . but seriously, Trudy is the *worst*!"

Mama giggled and hugged me again. "Ready for some spaghetti?"

In a span of two years, I learned my body didn't fit the ideal of two different sports. In gymnastics, I was too big and in soccer, I was too small. And even if it was just opinion, I was aware of my body in ways I had never considered in the past. For a girl who already felt she had to try *extra* hard to be validated and accepted, these ideals were difficult to overlook.

Mama's story helped as I battled opinions on my body. She gave me tools to empower me. And just as she encouraged me to do, I continued working hard in all the ways I knew how. Daily, after high school practice, I put in extra training at home. I went running to improve my endurance, and I kicked and juggled the soccer ball in the yard to improve my touch. By the end of the season, a local club soccer coach came to one of my high school games. He was there to cheer for my teammates who played for *his* team. After our game, the coach approached me and offered me a spot on his club team. I declined and told him my family couldn't afford the club fees. To my surprise, he offered me a full scholarship. It was a dream come true! I was getting a chance to play on a club soccer team. Ironically, I had a great season with that club team and ended up taking the starting position of the *same* girl who told me I was too small to play competitive soccer.

Mama's simple yet relatable "Costume Story" will remain one of my favorite stories she ever told me. Now, after all these years and as a lifelong athlete, I share with you that I have yet to outgrow the critiques and opinions about my appearance, but I lovingly say that I have used them for good. I welcome the questions and critiques about my size and powerful thighs as a professional runner. I want to have meaningful conversations and hopefully help others accept themselves just the way they are. It's not uncommon to learn that one of my critics is struggling with their *own* appearance or self-belief. Every time I stand on a start line, I'm making a strong statement. My hope, whether through my running or my words, is to encourage anyone struggling with self-worth, body image, or belief. I had a powerful Mama speaking into my life, guiding me to believe in myself, and reminding me to consistently work hard. Not everyone has someone like this in their life, so allow me to take a moment to be that to you, my friend.

Let's focus on what our bodies can do, and not on what they look like. Your body is shaped perfectly for you and the journey meant for you. Don't let anyone say you can't do what you love because of how you look. This is *your* life and no one can live it for you.

Embrace the *one* body you have.

Strengthen it.

Care for it.

Appreciate it.

Stand in it.

Unaltered and fully valid.

Mama in her dancing days

Poem for the Kids with Holes in their Shoes

With holes in your shoes,
you grew bolder.
You stood on the Start line next to
the expensive shoes,
the ones that sparkled.
Focused,
you locked your eyes on the course ahead.
You knew better.
When it was time,
you put your dirty shoe on the line;
and they looked you over.
But you ran with all your heart.
You ran alone.
You ran to the sound of *your* feet against the earth;
You bravely pushed through the discomfort.
And when you crossed the finish line in first place,
The crowds began to cheer.
Some whispered in bewilderment;
"Who's the odd girl over there?"
But you walked with your heart up;
No reason to cower.
You held the truth inside;
No material thing is greater than your value.

-yellowrunner

CHAPTER 10

CANCER

Danielle and Bonnie were my best friends in middle school and when we started high school together, we met Scott and Barry. Most of my favorite memories from high school were spent with these four. I fell hard for Scott, or most affectionately, Scotty. Scotty had electric blue eyes, wild hair, and a smile that I can still picture in my mind. Everyone loved his carefree personality, and he unknowingly set me at ease the moment I saw him.

Scotty and I talked on the phone most nights, and sometimes he bravely explained all the reasons he had feelings for me. One night, as we chatted, he told me to listen as he held the phone against his speaker system. I could hear him fumbling with the buttons on his CD player and then his voice came through in the background, "Okay, this is the song that reminds of you!" And for the next few minutes, I listened to Tom Petty's song, "Free Fallin.'" My face turned red as I listened. When it was over, I wished I could tell Scotty all the reasons I liked him, too, but I was terrified to let him get too close, even though I wanted him close. I liked Scotty more than I had ever liked anyone else. We loved all the same things—the beach, soccer, running, pugs, and writing each other long letters. My favorite thing about being with Scotty was how much he made me laugh. Although I could never explain it to him, his ability to make me smile cheered me up amid countless difficult and gloomy days.

Dad was strict about boys, clothes, and ear piercings. Ear piercings were out of the question because, according to Dad, it might "go out of style." The idea of *having a boyfriend* was both a mystery and a fear. By my understanding, it was the rule—no boyfriends, no kissing, no touching, nothing. I was raised with the idea I should only look for a person to marry and *that person* should be a church-going, morally good man. As I got older, I believed I'd go straight to hell if a boy ever laid hands on me.

I rarely invited friends to my house, and on the rare occasion they came for a visit, anxiety set in. The thought of a friend or me making the monster come out was unbearable. Unfortunately, this fear continued to shape how close I let people get to me.

From an observer's point of view, at fourteen years old, I was like many high school girls, trying to figure out where to fit in and how to keep up with a changing body, emotions, and the growing load of school work. I appeared to be a happy teenager, playing on the varsity soccer team, turning all my assignments in on time, and laughing during lunch with my friends.

Halfway through my freshman year, my brother, who had moved out of the house two years prior, came home for a weekend visit. He had only been home for a few hours when Dad said, "Everyone go sit at the dining room table." I was quick to examine my parents' facial expressions and tried figuring out whether one of us was in trouble. This was typically my first thought whenever Dad gathered us together. *Who was in trouble?* I questioned myself in these types of situations, then I evaluated my actions over the past week, wondering if I had done anything wrong.

One time, when I was nine years old, Dad told all five of us to sit on the couch. Someone had clogged the toilet, and he knew one of us did it (*on purpose, of course*). Mama stood anxiously next to him as he scanned our faces and snarled, "You better tell me who it is or I will whip all of you."

When no one responded, the monster held up a handful of candy canes and said, "If you confess, you will get all these candy canes."

No one loved candy more than me and I was confused about what the monster was doing, so I lied, "I did it! Now can I have the candy?" I can still see the desperate look on Mama's face when I spoke up, her fearful eyes knowing what would come next. The monster growled, "I KNEW IT! Go to your room Sally!"

I didn't clog the toilet, but I think the monster knew how much I liked candy. The real reason I volunteered to take the blame was because I didn't want one of my siblings getting whipped. I hated when they got in trouble and I couldn't stand listening to their punishment, or worse, watching it.

I wondered if this situation would be anything like the clogged-toilet incident. Light from the golden hour poured through the screen door, illuminating the back of Mama's head as she sat at the table. Dad stayed standing, which made my heart race. My brother sat across from me and looked somberly into my eyes as if he knew something. I shot him an intense look. *What? What do you know?* And then Dad's voice broke the silence, "Kids, we have some difficult news to share with you . . ."

Right away, I looked at Mama. Something wasn't right, and I didn't sense fear the same way I did when we were about to be *disciplined*. Mama's face looked sad. And then Dad continued, "Mom went to a doctor last week, and we received results from some tests they ran on her . . ." And then Dad's words slowed down, like molasses, and every syllable hung in the air.

My sisters shifted in their seats next to me, and I looked back at my brother, who looked like he was about to cry. *He knows what Dad is about to say!* And then Dad said it, the worst news in the universe exploded through the air, piercing our brains, "And she has *cancer*."

For a moment, no one moved, and then a spray of questions came from around the table, "What kind of cancer? What does that mean? Will she be okay?" I looked at Mama. Tears escaped down her cheeks and one by one, my sisters embraced her. I remained in my chair, trying to process the answers Dad was giving. "She has breast cancer and unfortunately, we found it too late. The doctors can't make Mama's cancer go away."

I hardened against the words and promised myself right there, from that day forward, I would never let Mama see me cry. She didn't need to worry about me. I was strong and I could be strong for her.

My siblings embraced Mama, and she looked at me as I stood from the table. I wanted to hug her, too. I wanted to cry and bury myself in her embrace, but I couldn't. Instead, I stood there, nailed to the floor.

It felt easier to harden myself against feelings because what I was feeling was agonizing. To my knowledge, I had never heard of a fourteen-year-old girl in my position. I had no guide, no example, no way of knowing what to do or what to think. The only time I had heard of a child losing a parent was in the movies, and those movies weren't real. Surely, this couldn't be real.

I lied to myself and I pushed the truth away.

She's not sick, she's gonna be okay.

This will soon end.

Mama will be healed.

She *needs* to be okay.

CHAPTER 11

LIE OR STAND UP

For most of my childhood, I waited for someone to rescue me when the monster was hurting me, but no one came. I blamed no one then, and I blame no one now. Everyone in the house would have saved me if they could, and I wish I could have saved them too, but we were helpless. We were trained to fear and respect the one who harmed us. But there was a light in the distance—at least that's what I envisioned in my mind. I hoped that if I kept getting off the floor, something better would await me. Hope without action is just daydreaming, but hope *with* action can move mountains. At fifteen years old, I took action.

One morning after the monster beat me, I waited on the floor until I heard his keys jingle. When the front door slammed and the sound of his engine was far enough down the street, I confronted Mom. "Why do you stay with him, Mama? I don't understand how you can stay with someone who hurts your children."

Surprised by my directness, Mama paused. I was confident that no one had ever asked her those questions. Sometimes, I wondered what she told her friends about our home life. Who did she talk to?

Anyone who got to know Mama loved her. She was a wonderful mother and friend. At Christmas, she made cookie plates for the neighbors and throughout the year, she sat at the kitchen table writing long cards to her friends back in Bonita Mesa. We always knew when a friend was visiting because she baked a special treat and worked to get the house extra clean. I wondered if Mama had a friend to whom she bared her soul. My friendships meant everything to me. Being with my friends was very important, and sharing laughs, embarrassing moments, and talking about the boys we liked made us feel closer to each other. I wondered if Mama hid information like I did. Like when I was in P.E. class in eighth grade and Danielle asked why I had handfuls of hair on the back of my shirt. I lied and told her I had brushed my hair hard trying to get a knot out. I lied because if I told her I was dragged down the hallway by my hair and beaten right before I left for the bus stop, it would make our friendship awkward. How was she supposed to respond? To fit in with the rest of the world, I kept the abuse hidden.

I imagined it was possible Mama kept secrets like I did. I kept things secret because I saw how the odd kids were treated at school—kids like Beth in my third grade class. She had extra-thick reading glasses and wore the same dirty pink jacket every day. Mama used to tell us to be kind and defend the kids who have no friends at school. She said we should never judge another kid because, "You don't know what their lives are like." So when the kids at school made fun of Beth because she smelled like cigarettes and her filthy hair was never brushed, I put my arm around her and said, "Don't listen to those stupid kids. I'm your friend."

Even then, at eight years old, I knew Beth hid her hurt like me. She rarely smiled and never took part in class. Whenever we played at recess, she spoke quietly because she didn't want the kids to hear her stutter. She seldom said a sentence without struggling. Sometimes she apologized to me for it and I told her not to be sorry. I smiled into her face and said, "Sometimes I stutter and I can't say the letter S, but that's okay!" And I'm sure it made her feel better. During class, our teacher, Mrs. Hughes, would bring her to the half-moon shaped table in the back of the classroom while the rest of us worked on our math worksheet. We could hear Mrs. Hughes talking gently to Beth about math that differed from the math we were learning. I don't think Beth did well because they put her in a different classroom halfway through the year—the one where no kids wanted to go because then you were made fun of for being *dumb*. I was sad when Beth and I were no longer in class together, and I was even more sad when she told me she was moving before the school year was over. I remember not knowing what to say the last day I saw her, so I said, "I'm gonna miss you Beth. I hope you always know you are beautiful."

Throughout my life, I have never forgotten Beth. I wondered why she made such an impact on me when in reality, there was no particular thing she did to inspire me. But maybe that's just it. Maybe she impacted me because of who she was and that was *enough*. Unlike my other childhood friendships, I had a special connection with Beth—one maybe she didn't know about. I could *feel* her heartache and I understood her sadness. We were so much alike, except I didn't wear my abuse for the world to see. I brushed my hair and wore clean clothes and when people talked to me, I smiled and held interesting conversations. And when I went to the special class for speech therapy, most kids didn't know. If they found out, I lied and said I was going to the class for *extra* smart kids.

Beth impacted me because she was visibly beaten down for all to see and yet every day she showed up at school. She didn't try to impress anyone and she didn't try to be someone she wasn't. She was dirty and stinky and outcast, and she sat right there with us.

I'm not sure if Beth remembers me. It's been three decades since I last saw her, but Beth, if by some miracle you are reading this today, I want you to know I meant what I said on that last day I saw you. "You are beautiful, and I miss you."

I didn't know if Mama had anyone to talk to. I waited anxiously for Mama's response and she explained she thought about leaving Dad many times throughout their marriage, but she had nowhere to go and no money to live independently from Dad. Bitterness built inside me as she spoke. How had Mama felt trapped for so long? She looked away briefly, trying hard not to cry. I responded with urgency, "I would rather live in the car than with him! And I can make money. I know how to work, you know that. I can work real hard, Mama!"

Mama's sad eyes met mine and she explained how Dad told her if she left him, he would come find her—and when he did, she would be sorry. He said she had nothing without him, and he questioned her ability to make enough money to care for five children. I sat, dumbfounded by her response, and then she added, "You know your dad is a really great husband. He has always loved me well. Being a dad is hard sometimes. He's not a good dad." I wasn't expecting the "he's a great husband" part, and I wrestled to understand how a man could be a great husband *and* an abusive father. What level of brainwashing does a woman need to go through to believe the husband who physically and verbally beats down her children is, in fact, a good husband?

Before we could finish our conversation, my sister walked in and surveying Mom's and my serious faces, stayed quiet. I wasn't comfortable talking about these issues in front of my sisters. I already felt separated by the way I was treated. Dad made it clear who his favorites were—he proclaimed it confidently in front of all five children one morning while we sat in the dining room. I wasn't on that list. And even then, being in grade school, I wasn't surprised. The saying, "Actions speak louder than words," is true for all time.

Mama sensed we were done, and she stood from where she was sitting, but I followed her from the room, intent on asking her one more question. "How much more are you gonna take of this, Mama? It isn't right. This is abuse!" It was the first time I called it what it was and the words coming from my mouth stunned Mama. Her face scrunched into a mess of worry. She was no longer dealing with a naïve child. I was growing up, and getting wiser, constantly surveying and figuring out how to survive in a world that felt like it was built on lies. Every relationship I had required me to be a liar. I lied to my friends about why I was having a bad day and pretended to be happy when inside, I was hurting. I knew the difference between right and wrong, and I was weary of the wrong. She paused and her chin quivered. I believe she, too, was desperate inside. Now, as a mother myself, I ache writing this part, imagining the anguish a mother feels when she can't protect her children.

Mama whispered now, "Sally, I'm sick. I have to stay. I wish he didn't hurt you. Please stay off his radar and don't make him upset . . . you have to stay out of his way."

Mama reminding me of her cancer made me feel horrible about bringing up the topic. I had judged her and I was sorry. Mama's idea of surviving an abusive relationship was to become invisible. Was this how she endured the relationship over the years? It made sense. Dad controlled the money and the direction of our family, not Mom. I questioned her statement that he was a "good husband," because it was common to hear him insult her—both to her face and when she wasn't around. Dad called Mama *fat* and *lazy*. And anytime I heard it, I squeezed my fists with anger.

Not a year went by when Mama wasn't trying a new diet or exercise program. When she complained about her need to lose weight, I wondered why? When you're young and you don't understand the concept of weight and fat, you infer your mom's discontent as a rejection of *self*. Even as a little girl, I remember feeling sad that Mama didn't see herself the way I saw her. She was beautiful, and I repeatedly told her she was pretty. I wrote it on cards and sticky notes. I complimented her outfits, her hair, and her bright pink lipstick. I loved her just the way she was.

Naturally, when Dad put her down, I was defensive. Dad was good at telling his family lies about themselves—and he told these lies so much that eventually, we believed them as truth.

Stand Up

"It's easy to feel stuck when you believe
you are weak and helpless.
It's easy to endure another day of abuse
when you believe you deserve it.
It's easy to be blinded from your worth when the
one you love makes you feel worthless.
At some point,
You must choose;
To stand up;
Or stay stuck.
At some point,
You must believe,
You ARE STRONG,
You are not helpless.
Stand up,
Stand up,
Stand up."

-yellowrunner

CHAPTER 12

WORK, LOVE, AND VEGETABLE JUICE

A few months after Mama's diagnosis, Tony's Italian Restaurant opened in the new strip mall down the street from our neighborhood. My older sister got a job there as a hostess and each night after her shift she brought home a quart of spumoni ice cream. I stole spoonfuls from her as I sat at the kitchen counter, listening to her entertaining stories about what happened at work that night. As soon as I was able, I excitedly applied for a position at the restaurant and joined my sister wearing black pants, a white button-up shirt, and a green apron.

Getting a *proper* job sounded grown up, and the idea of having a weekly paycheck was everything I thought I needed. I still babysat in the neighborhood on a weekly basis, but I was ready for something new, and another opportunity to be out of the house swayed me. More and more, I didn't like being at home, and if I was at home, I stayed in my room or busied myself with unnecessary chores. I was at peace with life if I stayed occupied, and it didn't matter if I had company. I liked working alone and I enjoyed the mundane moments on my hands and knees scrubbing the black scuffs off the white linoleum tile in the kitchen. Oddly, I felt protected while working. After all, if I was mowing the lawn or scrubbing a toilet, why would I get in trouble? Doing chores, especially without being instructed, brought about a comment of approval and I enjoyed being approved.

I didn't complain about working. I enjoyed making my own money. I bought the clothes and shoes I wanted, and I could finally afford nicer soccer cleats so I fit in with the rest of the girls on my team. The more time I spent away from home, the less I saw the monster. I controlled my world by working, and my world needed to be moving at all times. *Hard work* and *giving my best* didn't mean what it meant to other kids my age who hung the phrases on posters in their comfortable bedrooms. No, these phrases were how I survived. Hard work was how I was going to change my life.

At home, Mama was learning to battle the illness taking over her body. She rarely let us see or hear the pain she endured mentally and physically. Like many mothers, she was devoted to focusing on the needs of her family and savoring the moments she had with her children.

We were approved for Medi-Cal (*a free or low-cost health coverage for California residents who meet eligibility requirements*). After never having medical insurance, Mama could finally get the treatment she needed to care for her dying body. Back then, there was no such thing as online giving campaigns to help pay for someone's medical bills and social media didn't exist. The only people who knew about Mom's illness were the people who were *real* in our lives—like our neighbors, church friends, and our extended family and friends.

Mom's case was a rare and devastating situation—rare because she was at a terminal stage before the age of forty and devastating because, according to doctors, it could have been detected and treated several *years earlier* had she visited a doctor. But regular doctor visits weren't possible for our family of seven, and although we had newly qualified for free healthcare, it was too late.

In my anxiousness, I asked her questions about her diagnosis, "Why didn't you know sooner? Are you in pain right now? You don't look sick—are you sure the doctors are right? I think God will heal you. Do you believe that, too?"

I was searching for hope—a loophole to change the nightmare. I still remember our conversation in the kitchen as she pulled out a Tupperware box full of supplements. She was required to ingest a pile of pills each morning. It was a beautiful Saturday morning and the sliding doors and kitchen windows were wide open, revealing the blue desert sky. The family was eating breakfast and bustling around the house, getting ready for a day of sports when I paused next to her at the counter while she swallowed another pill, "Will those pills heal you?"

She responded, "Well, they will help me live longer." I bit my tongue and watched as she set the new vegetable juicer the doctor asked her to buy, on the countertop. Mom and Dad couldn't get over how expensive the machine was, but concluded if the doctor said it would help, then it would be worth every penny. She pulled beets, carrots, broccoli, spinach, and several other vegetables I hated from the fridge. In all my years as a kid, I had *never* seen so many fresh fruits and vegetables in our kitchen all at once. If we had fruit, it was apples and occasionally, we had bananas or oranges. The only veggies I liked were carrots and celery—the most commonly found vegetables in our fridge—and now and then Mom steamed broccoli or turnips, both of which made me want to gag with their dirt aroma and mushy texture.

Our grocery list was on repeat for most of my childhood, mainly because Mama was given a tight budget. With so many mouths to feed, she needed to find the most food for the least amount of money. So instead of real sandwich bread, we had sandwich *slices*, and instead of real cheese, we had American *slices*—which were basically hardened oil that had been dyed yellow and wrapped in cellophane. The word *slices* was a sign the product was a substitute for the real thing. Mom routinely bought beef—a two pound, mushy log that had been squeezed from a machine into a plastic casing. The tubes had different percentages written on them, 20/80, 15/85 or 7/93. When I asked Mom why she always bought the 20/80 meat, she said it was a better deal and that the numbers had to do with fat content—the more fat in the meat, the cheaper the price. Mom also bought, in my opinion, the most disgusting cereal. We weren't allowed to have sugary cereal and with five kids, a box of cereal was gone in one morning, so Mama bought the bulk bags of puffed rice and store brand versions of corn flakes and wheat squares. I used to complain about the sack lunches we brought to grade school, "Everyone else has Oreos and Cheetos, Mama." And she would remind me, "You have more food than most people and you know we can't afford that stuff."

Unlike the other kids at the lunch tables, no one wanted to trade food with me, and no one else had to bring home their used sandwich baggies and paper bags to be used again. But sometimes, the kids who brought full lunchboxes of brightly covered packages would toss me a bag. "Want my Doritos?" And I'd excitedly break open the bag, devouring every crumb of the foreign chips. As I got older, eating food at my friends' houses was one of my favorite things to do—they always had exciting snacks in their cupboards and soda in their refrigerators.

Occasionally, we had ice cream in the freezer and any time it rained, Mama baked her favorite spice cookies, which always made the house smell like Christmas. Mama said she loved the rain because we rarely got it in Southern California and the gray skies brought her peace as she mixed flour and sugar in a bowl.

But now, as I stood watching her wash and chop vegetables, I inquired about food, "What are you going to make with all those vegetables?" She glanced at me with a smile as she flipped the machine on and said, "Pure vegetable juice." The loud motor vibrated the kitchen counters as she shoved piece after piece of veggies into the chute. Beneath the spout, Mom placed a glass to catch the juice as the vegetables were squeezed into pulp. The smell made my face scrunch up, and Mom laughed, "Do you want to try it?"

I giggled back at her with big eyes, "No thanks!" She flipped the machine off and held up a murky colored glass of juice. I couldn't help but comment, "That looks like vomit Mama. How does that help you?"

Mom took a drink and then responded, "The doctor said I should eat as many fresh foods as possible and to load up on vegetable juice. He said it's good for fighting cancer."

I watched her finish the juice and commended her for drinking the most disgusting liquid I had ever seen in my life. In the days following, books on cancer and diet popped up around the house. Mom explained how she learned that processed foods and sugar were bad for the body and contributed to cancer growth. And again, in my anxiousness, I asked more questions, "How come we didn't know about the bad foods sooner? Do you think you wouldn't have cancer if you were juicing before? It sounds like you can't eat anything like you used to eat! Is everything *we* eat bad?" Mom continued listening to my relentless questions, answering them with tenderness, knowing her daughter was trying to navigate through the situation.

As my freshman year ended, Mom's treatments at the City of Hope hospital became routine. In the few months since she told us her diagnosis, she underwent a double-mastectomy and began chemotherapy and radiation. I knew little about her appointments, but she continually told the family how grateful she was to be chosen for treatment at this hospital, a well known not-for-profit clinical research center which was the leader in cancer research. According to her, every doctor and nurse showed her kindness and she assured us that when her hair fell out, she would get to pick out a nice wig.

Hearing Mom talk about hair loss and radiation treatments made my hands sweat, and I'd breathe a little faster if ever she mentioned something hurt. Most days, she went to her appointments while we were at school or out with friends, and when we arrived home, she was in bed sleeping. Sometimes, a nurse came over and gave her the treatments while she lay in bed. I never went in the room, but sometimes I pressed my ear against the wall for a chance to hear her. I didn't want to see what they were doing to her—I couldn't stand the sight of needles or even the idea that she was lying there helpless, as they routinely made her feel discomfort. Some days, she was more sick than others, and because she didn't want us to see her weak, it was difficult to understand how much she was enduring. She still went to church and to our sporting events, and she did her best to prepare dinner and listen to us whenever we needed to talk.

But when her hair started falling out, I saw the light in her eyes change. I always loved Mama's dark wavy hair and the small curls that formed near the sides of her forehead, especially on rainy days. My hair was straight and flat and I told her I wished I had hair like hers. She laughed and bantered back, "Well, I always wanted straight hair like yours! I used to iron my hair in high school. I guess we are never happy with what we got!"

Seeing her sad made me sad, and I envisioned what it would be like if all my hair fell out. Sometimes, on nights when I couldn't fall asleep, I got mad at God. Hot tears streamed into my pillow as I clenched my jaw and protested, "Why my mama? Why are you doing this to her? What wrong did she do?"

I hated that nothing made sense. There was nothing I could do to make her better, and I especially hated that windy Sunday afternoon when I was home alone. I hadn't joined my family at the church picnic because I needed to get ready for work. While I was in Mama's bathroom brushing my hair, I heard the front door slam and simultaneously loud weeping coming down the hallway. I ran to meet her and the shock on her face turned to embarrassment. "I thought you were already at work."

I asked Mama why she was upset and she nervously walked toward the bathroom and took off her pink baseball cap. A loosely tied bandana was still on her bald head as she explained, "We were at the church picnic and I was sitting in my chair when a gust of wind blew off my hat and bandana. Everyone just stared at me! I was so embarrassed just sitting there with my bald head . . . it's so ugly . . . no one said anything. I just left."

Overcome with sadness and anger, I pulled her close to me and hugged her. Her body felt smaller than it used to in my arms. "I wish I could have been there for you. I would have run so fast to get your hat, Mama!" Comforting words seemed to come easily for Mama whenever I was sad and I searched for words to ease her, just as she had done for me countless times. "I love you." I didn't know what else to say, and Mama's anguish and embarrassment seemed to consume her as she made her way to her bed. I watched her for a moment, feebly fighting off guilt as I wrestled with my need to work and my longing to stay with her until she fell asleep. But I didn't know how to stay and I didn't want to feel all those feelings longer than I already had. I needed to work like I needed to breathe, so I walked out the front door and left Mama alone in her room, telling myself that she was going to be okay.

CHAPTER 13

COURAGE

In my experience in ultra running, I've learned it takes *courage* to stand on the start line. We don't need much, but when rooted in *belief* and *hope*, that courage is unstoppable. The mind is an unmatched source of strength in overcoming challenges—far greater than the physical body. People who toe the start line of an ultra distance do so because they *believe* they can get to the finish line. These courageous souls also know that uncontrollable obstacles await them—obstacles that come in the form of physical discomfort, mental fatigue, self-doubt, injury, changes in weather, faulty gear, or getting lost on the trail, to name a few. Still, these athletes go anyway, ready to take on the journey with hope for the finish line. *Ultimately, the discomfort is worth the prize.*

A few months before my sixteenth birthday, I was given a sturdy introduction to courage and it changed my life. The word *courage* derives from the Latin word *cor*, which means "the heart." Originally, courage was defined, "To speak one's mind by revealing all one's heart." In simpler terms, it meant "to speak openly and to act honestly with integrity." The following story, although difficult to retell, is my first lesson in choosing courage in the face of fear. My decision to act honestly out of love was scary because I knew it would be painful. I weighed the physical pain against my love for Mama. Love was greater—it always is.

One afternoon, while I did homework in my bedroom, the phone rang. Mama answered it and I could hear her murmur a few words and then go quiet, so I wandered from my room out of curiosity. Her worried face alerted me and when she said, "I don't understand why you didn't bring the soccer balls with you?" I could immediately hear his familiar snarl growling back into the phone. Mama's face went limp and she hung up. Anxious about the call, I asked, "What's going on, Mama? What did he say?"

She hurried to the garage, and I followed closely behind. I watched as she fumbled with an oversized bag of soccer balls. I sensed fear in her voice as she said, "I'm warning you right now Sally, he is *very* angry."

Mama's hair had started growing back, but every time I looked at her, I saw an invisible sign that read, "I'm ill." Mama wasn't as physically strong as she used to be, but she tried her best. I wish the monster saw her the way I did, with compassion.

The doctors said she was in a season of partial remission. Supposedly, this meant she got a break from a bald head and the merciless symptoms of chemotherapy, but Mama didn't hide the truth from us. We knew the cancer was still there and it wouldn't be long before it came back in a severe way. Worried, I asked more questions, "Why is he angry? What's he gonna do?"

I helped Mama haul the bag to the living room and she replied, "I just need to get these soccer balls to him. He's late to coach soccer practice. I only said he should have brought the balls with him so he could go straight from work to practice and now he's . . . he's furious."

My mind raced, envisioning how the scene would play out once the monster stepped into the house. All signs pointed to hostility, and knowing he was driving closer to home with each passing minute put pressure on me. I *needed* to do something. Mama was worth defending and I thought about the number of times the monster had hit me—*countless*. An idea formed in my head, one that was worth the resulting pain. Something needed to change, and I gave myself two options—choose to be courageous or choose to be afraid.

I walked to the screen door, waiting for the familiar sound of the brown van. Within seconds, it appeared. I clenched my fists and inhaled a deep, shaky breath just as Mama walked up behind me. "Sally, what are you doing?" A justified anger pulsated through my veins and I pushed open the screen door and stepped outside. Mama hurried in front of me and frantically demanded, "Sally, get back in the house. You're gonna make him mad . . . Sally!"

We could feel the intensity building as the monster pulled halfway into the driveway and I firmly responded, "I'm not gonna let him hurt you."

Seconds later, the monster came charging around the corner and screamed, "YOU BITCH! HOW DARE YOU SPEAK TO ME THAT WAY!"

I maneuvered ahead and anchored myself in front of Mama right before the monster reached her. Our eyes met, and I scowled into his gray eyes and yelled, "DON'T CALL *MY MOM* A BITCH!" My body tightened as I heard my own words—there was no backing down now. I knew what would happen next.

In the past, Mama downplayed the monster's violent behavior and made up excuses for his erratic outbursts. I still remember lying in my bunk bed the night he threw the coffee table across the living room. It crashed into the wall just above her head. I flinched and cried angry tears as I listened to the chaos on the other side of my bedroom wall. When I awoke in the morning, I went to the living room to find her sitting on the couch and a large rectangular hole in the wall behind her. I gasped at the sight of it, "Mama! Did he throw the table at you?!" The answer was more than obvious, but I *needed to hear* her response. I needed to know that *she* knew it was wrong.

Instead, she hushed me, "It looks worse than it is. It's not a big deal. Everything is fine now. Don't say anything about it."

And that was it. We didn't discuss those incidents. Truth in my family was swept under the rug. Ignoring the truth kept the already tense environment from exploding, or so I thought. Instead, things were now exploding in front of me. Mama was precious, but I don't know if she believed that about herself.

I'm sure you can imagine the monster's reaction—no one had ever stood up to him, and he was going to make sure it never happened again. His voice boomed, "What!? You think you can talk to me like that, you spoiled brat!" And with a single lunge, he yanked me by my shirt and forced me into the house.

Mama begged, "Stop it! NO! STOP!" As soon as I was thrown to the floor, the weight of his body pressed me into the ground and, just as I expected, his first hit shook my core. But I had already planned my reaction. I calculated his hits, and spoke to myself—*The first one will hurt the worst, but then you'll know what to expect.*

I can *feel* Mama at this moment. A mother, completely helpless to her hurting child, is far more tortured than if the pain was inflicted on her. I now understand why she wanted me to stay out of sight, because to her, it was the *only* way she knew to protect me. Had I stayed quietly in my room, Mama wouldn't have had to watch the very act that brought her pain all those years.

Change was taking place, and the monster knew it. I had no respect for him and for the first time I realized, although he was twice my size and easily overpowered my physical body, he couldn't touch my mind. I was strong—even though I was beneath him. He didn't know what I was thinking and he couldn't control how I responded. I was the master of my mind, *not* him! I continued talking through his pathetic thrashing. *It won't last long . . . that one is done . . . here it comes again . . . hang on Sally . . . stay strong.*

The monster had one goal—to inflict pain and fear so I would never stand up to him again. But I had learned his ways. I was studious, and earlier that year, I went as far as to ask Mama why he was particularly cruel to me. Mama said the monster believed in breaking our spirits because it would make us more obedient children. She said the monster wanted us to fear him and that I was "the hardest one to break," so I usually received the harshest punishments. I'll *never* forget that twisted conversation. Initially, I had mixed emotions about it, but I also held an odd sense of pride knowing the monster was aware of my resiliency. But, it didn't make sense- he was my dad; why did he want to break my spirit? I guess a lot of things don't make sense when we're kids, but there are also lingering things that make little sense even into our adult years. This is one of them.

When he finally finished, he glared at Mama and blamed her for raising a disrespectful child. Then he pointed into my face and barked, "See what happens when you challenge me!"

I stayed on the ground as he scurried out the door. Mama knelt next to me, crying, and asked, "Sally, are you okay?" Slowly assessing the marks on my body, I sat up and found Mama's bloodshot eyes looking back at me.

"I didn't want him to hurt you, Mama." Overcome with emotion, my whole body shook. *What just happened?* I squeezed

Mama, and she continued to cry, but then hardness set in. I was full of rage. Even though I wanted to stay, I aimlessly ran to the backyard and wheeled my bike toward the gate.

Mama followed, bewildered, and called to me, "Wait . . . where are you going?"

I bit back, "Away from here!"

Like an out-of-body experience, rage put me on that bike seat and I pedaled ferociously down the street. I cycled with such fury I thought for sure I'd crash. I wanted to stay, but I didn't know how. I rode into the hills across the street from our neighborhood. People rarely took that dirt path. My emotions swung like a pendulum from pride for standing up to the monster to choking on remorse, thinking of my dying Mama. I was courageous and angry. I was brave and helpless. And now I hated that I was alone in the middle of nowhere. Why had I pushed away the one person who was there to comfort me? Exhausted, I stopped pedaling and angrily shoved my bike to the ground. I hated the monster and wished he was the one who was sick. I wanted every painful, tortuous feeling Mama had endured to be put on the monster.

I screamed into the cold desert air, "You weak asshole! Think you can hurt me?! I'll stand up to you! You piece of shit! I HATE YOU! I HATE YOU!"

The sun began to set, and I wearily dropped to the ground and scanned the horizon. I watched as the sun hit a mass of clouds and sunk behind the hills. A gentle breeze brushed my skin, and I knew if I didn't leave soon, I'd be riding home in the dark. Arriving home before Dad was crucial and so I stood up and wiped the dust from my clothes. My energy had dwindled and my legs felt heavy as I pedaled toward the main road.

Turning into my neighborhood, a friendly neighbor watering his lawn waved to me. I smiled and waved back. He had no idea what had happened just hours before, and oddly, that realization calmed me. My abuse was hidden, my pain unknown. Pedaling closer to my house, I spotted my friend Ryan tossing a baseball in the air, catching it with ease as he chatted with his dad, who was tinkering in the garage. I didn't want Ryan to see me. I anxiously searched the front of my house and thankfully, only Mama's beat up station wagon was parked out front. In one motion, I hopped off my moving bike and jogged to the side of the house. I breathed out a sigh of relief as I pushed my bike through the side gate and as soon as I stepped inside, Mama was there waiting with a sad look on her face. "Where did you go, Sally? I was so worried about you."

I wanted her to know I was sorry for leaving and wrapped my arms around her neck and whispered, "I'm sorry Mama. I just needed to go."

She released her embrace to survey me and said, "It's okay. I *really* hate what happened to you today . . . I wasn't expecting you to do that. I just need to know if you're okay?"

Her expression made my eyes water, and I whispered, "I'm glad I did it, and yes, I'm okay. I love you . . . I promise I'm okay."

Unlike earlier, I wasn't filled with anger and fear. A new feeling was taking root inside me—*courage*. Things didn't change overnight. I still had a lot to work through, but a seed was planted and it's been growing ever since. I stopped writing this book for many years because of this story, but I courageously share it with you today, knowing that whether you are searching for the courage to stand up for good or courage to sign up for a race, it's common for discomfort to follow. It's difficult to write that, knowing that isn't what you want to hear when talking about courage, but the difference between what we want to hear and what is true is what helps us move toward the best outcomes in life. I also think it's important to point out that when I talk about pain and courage in life, it can *look* strikingly different than pain and courage in a race.

In 2003, CBS News posted an online article by the brilliant neuroscientist, Robert Coghill, Ph.D, titled: "Pain is Relative." It's short, but you might find it interesting along with some of his other studies on pain and how powerful our brains can be in helping us endure it. There's one particularly interesting study where all ten people who participated in a pain perception study had lessened pain intensity when they *expected* lower levels of pain. This study wasn't around when I was a kid and reading it today struck a chord with me because it's similar to how I worked through pain as a child. Inevitably, I still use this strategy today while racing. I expect discomfort and I expect setbacks to thwart my efforts on race day, but not in a pessimistic way. I have a plan for every possible situation long before I stand on the start line. Preparation isn't as exciting as the actual event we prepare for, but preparation is a powerful factor in helping us get to the finish line. It's important to add here that expecting discomfort without the presence of hope can, over time, put us into a negative mindset, something I also experienced as a child. I am not one to chase down the feelings of pain and suffering but I am perpetually curious about human limits. What if, instead of being surprised or embittered when things don't go our way, we instead train and prepare ourselves to be ready for everything? What if we took everything we learned in sport and competition and applied it to life?

When I raced Badwater 135 in 2021, I created a training plan with a greater focus on mental training and tactics than I did when I raced Badwater for the first time in 2018. After experiencing significant physical discomfort from Miles 30–135 in 2018, I finished the race determined to discover what tools I was lacking to have the race in which I knew I was capable. I wanted to win and I knew I wasn't lacking in fitness, experience, or high pain tolerance, which led me to studying my mind.

During my preparation in 2021, I studied everything I could find on heat training, nutrition and hydration, ideal clothing and colors in extreme heat, and so on. I listened to podcasts and watched science professors on YouTube lecture on various topics related to physical and mental training in endurance events. Over time, I gathered loads of invaluable takeaways, but there was no study on Sally McRae running 135 miles through Death Valley in the dead of summer where temperatures rise to 130°F. Halfway into my training block, I experienced a rejuvenated excitement in discovering what works best for me and me uniquely. For almost two months before race day, I traveled to different locations where temperatures scorched the pavement between 105–125°F. I kept a notebook and logged how I felt during long and short training runs in the exposed heat. What I was able to digest at 105°F compared to 125°F was very different; and my running paces, and perceived exertion also changed as the temperature increased.

I took note of my mental state and whether or not my mind wandered to negative or positive thinking. During long training sessions on the race course, I allowed myself to think deeply about every possible race day malfunction. From there, I worked tediously to find a solution for every situation. Did I need additional gear or supplies? What if no material thing could solve my discomfort—what words would I say to myself to keep me moving? I thought about the level of physical pain each situation would cause me, for example, how does the pain of a blister compare to hours of vomiting? What would I do if I had a headache or if I pulled a muscle? Perhaps race day would hit record breaking temperatures (like it did in 2018). Would I need to change my pacing and eating strategy? What would I do if my crew van got a flat tire or got stuck in the sand? For weeks I mulled over dozens of scenarios, all the while staying hopeful of my goal and envisioning myself running those final steps through the finish line into first place. The mental training and experimenting I did on myself leading up to the race proved to be the most important factors in my victory. Expecting discomfort as part of race day gave me greater control of my reactions. The truth is, *every runner* on that course was experiencing some degree of pain and discomfort. It's just as much a part of the race as the elation and joy of finishing that brutal course.

The pain I experienced in standing up to the monster was very different from the pain I felt in Badwater 135. I am grateful to come out the other side of *all* my experiences with a stronger perspective. I can take what I have learned in life and apply it to a race, but I can also take what I learn in a race and apply it to life. Pain is a part of our journey and it takes strength and courage to move forward despite it. I believe we are built to stand strong for each other. Personally, I want a life filled with lots of standing, whether I'm standing at the start line of a 100-mile race or standing to defend a loved one—standing in strength and courage is a life worth living.

Courage over fear. Me(15) and Mama (41) standing strong together.

Registration for Pain

Running an ultramarathon is *not* pain and suffering.
Pushing through cramping, body aches, and nausea isn't detrimental.
Running up mountains, through desserts and inclement
weather isn't the hardest thing I will do in life.
These things started with a choice.
I chose an opportunity to push my physical limits.
No one dragged me to the start line.
When the race was over,
I could learn from my mistakes *and* my triumphs.
The races and adventures I choose in life are gifts.
As a lifelong athlete and someone who *gets to* do sport as a career,
I am grateful for how sports gently allow
us to push through discomfort.
But throughout my life,
I have known the pain of being dragged into
nightmarish events I didn't sign up for.
Aid stations, supportive crews, and the opportunity to DNF,
did not exist.
These moments have shaped me into the woman I am today.
There is a difference between
the discomfort we choose and the pain we are forced to endure.
These words are for those standing in the wilderness,
Far away from the start lines of recreational activities.
To the dear hearts navigating a pain that didn't
come with a registration form.
I SEE you.
Your pain matters;
You matter.
Stand strong
and courageous.
You're not done yet.

-yellowrunner

CHAPTER 14

UNSTABLE GROUND

After standing up to the monster, the environment changed but not entirely as a direct result of my rebellion. This poignant event was quickly followed by a series of days filled with "bad news." Dad started battling a mysterious illness, finances got noticeably tighter, and through the walls, I heard my parents discuss missed house payments. To top it off, Mama's short-lived partial remission ended.

It was no secret that time with Mom was limited, but I didn't allow myself to think about it. I did what I knew best and stayed busy. Purple and blue bruises popped up on Mama's skin more frequently, a visible reminder of her weakened immune system. She tried to stay occupied and moved around the house as she usually did—doing chores, running errands, and visiting with friends.

Dad was stressed. Driving from the desert to the coast, the two hours of messy round trip traffic was taking its toll. Since most of Dad's contract work was around Bonita Mesa, he had no choice but to make the commute. It was the one way he knew to provide an honest income, so he persevered.

From the time I was old enough to understand the concept of money, finances were tight in our home. But now the debt was worse than ever before and my understanding of it increased my anxiety. During this time, Dad frequently battled intense migraines. Sometimes during dinner, Dad finished eating and dropped his head onto his crossed arms right there at the dining room table. It became so frequent, I started whispering my concerns to Mama, "Is he okay? Why are his headaches so bad?" Dad stayed at the table for what seemed like an hour and Mama told us to let him rest, assuring us he was dealing with stress and would be okay—but it was obvious he was not well.

A couple months later, I finished my sophomore year and just as my sisters and I settled into what we hoped would be a summer with friends and trips to the beach, we were given bad news—we lost our home. My parents could no longer keep up with the monthly house payments and the foreclosure process had already begun.

When our parents said we were moving back to our hometown in Bonita Mesa, I went to my room and cried bitterly into my pillow. Imagining life without Bonnie, Danielle, Barry, and Scotty was painful. I didn't want to move back. I loved my friends and my soccer team and couldn't imagine having to start all over again at a new school. Like salt to an already exposed wound, losing our home while Mama's health declined stung.

I took soccer posters off my painted green walls and folded my favorite overalls and oversized flannels into a box. When my bedroom door was closed late at night, I unleashed my emotions through journal entries and sifted through pictures of Bonnie, Danielle, and me. Their smiles and unconditional friendship toward me highlighted my years in middle school and high school. My heart ached as I picked up pictures of Scotty and Barry. I would miss their daily bantering and the way they made me laugh, no matter how terrible my day was. I sighed, regretting all the parts about myself I kept hidden from my friends. Some days I wondered if they guessed my secrets. We were all close, but I knew I could never be as close to them as they were to each other. I didn't want them to become a distant memory, but did I have a choice? The shoebox holding the letters they passed me in between classes was my greatest treasure. I smiled at Scotty's hilarious drawings of us driving around town in his beat up Omni, and re-read Danielle and Bonnie's colorful notes about nothing and everything. It was all ending too suddenly.

The time between when our move was announced and the moving truck arrived felt painfully short. I focused on the boxes instead of my warring feelings and lied to myself saying we would be back often to visit. I remember staring at the tall sunflowers as we drove from the house for the last time. Mama had lovingly planted them beneath the front windows. I didn't know sunflowers could grow so tall. I also didn't know I could simultaneously love and despise a house so much. That black and white house was my home from the ages of ten to sixteen—a home I remember with equal parts joy and pain.

I kept quiet, leaned my head against the window, and stared at the open fields in the distance as we made our way to the freeway. Mom sensed the sadness radiating from her daughters, and just as she always did, tried to find the light in the situation. "You know the good thing is we will go back to the same church and be close to our old friends again."

It was hard to argue with Mama when she was sick, and this was the absolute sickest we had seen her. The color in her skin looked different and her eyes sunk a bit more into her face. Her physical strength was declining and even though she tried to carry her own weight with the move, she wasn't able to lift things like she used to. Listening to her talk about what awaited us in Bonita Mesa made my mind wander. I didn't want to hear about it.

After two hours of driving, we parked on the street in a crowded neighborhood. I stepped from our old maroon station wagon and stared at an ugly apartment, which I guessed was our new home. It was a plain structure with two units attached to the back. I bit my tongue as I followed Mama through the front door and into the entryway. The ceilings were low, and every corner looked dark. I had an intense dislike for dark rooms, and I knew Mama did, too. I looked at her face as we made our way to the grossly outdated kitchen and sensed she was mustering up a positive outlook for the rest of us.

Mama raised me to be thankful, but I didn't want to be grateful for *anything* at that moment. I wanted to complain and yell about all the drastic changes. I followed Mama into the living room and when I caught sight of her bruised, frail arms, a wave of guilt smacked me square in the face. This apartment would likely be where Mama would spend her last days, and here I was, brewing in bitterness.

I feigned positivity, "This is a nice space, Mama, and look at the fireplace!" Hoping to make her believe I was content, I walked over to the living room window and opened the blinds, letting the light fill the room. Undoubtedly, the move was difficult for her, too, but she kept quiet about it that day.

Dad walked into the room, and my sisters followed. I studied their somber faces and listened as Dad explained his plan to stay in the apartment for six months while he looked for a house to rent. Relieved, I flashed a smile at Mama hoping it was true. Looking for a home for six people and a dog on short notice proved to be more challenging than Mom and Dad expected, so unlike me, they were grateful for the apartment.

Mama got a job caring for babies at our church across the street from the apartment. One of her best friends was the nursery director and thoughtfully gave her a couple of three-hour shifts. Those shifts meant a lot to Mama. Rocking babies to sleep and chatting with her friends was a gift she looked forward to every week. Mama held the job before we moved to Rock City, so returning to it after all these years brought a happiness to her I hadn't seen in a while.

With only a few weeks before school started, I asked my parents to help me find a club soccer team. I knew we couldn't afford the fees, but now that I was aware of scholarships, I planned to ask every team in the area for financial help. As a junior in high school, I felt the pressure of what is historically known as the most important year in the recruiting process. I needed to be on a club team to be seen.

A premier level team (at this time, *premier* was the highest level in club soccer) was hosting try-outs for two spots. It wasn't until I arrived at the field that I learned most of the girls were seventeen and eighteen years old—it was an older team. At sixteen, I was the youngest one on the field. If I made the team, I'd have consistent exposure to college scouts. A wave of insecurity jabbed at me while I sat on the grass outside the circle of girls. I fumbled with my shin guards and shoelaces, listening to them banter with each other like old friends.

After searching for teams in the area with open spots, this was my only chance to get on a club team. I needed to make a choice—let my insecurity get the best of me or believe I deserved to be there. Standing up to join the team for warm-ups, I chose to give 110 percent. Speed and grit were my greatest strengths, so I needed to highlight those as best I could. If I went up against a girl with fancy footwork, she would likely get around me, but I was scrappy. I could chase anyone down, and with a step ahead and a swerve of my hips, I'd push hard into an opponent to steal the ball. Nothing fired me up more than scoring, and historically, I was one of the top scorers on all my teams.

As we moved through practice, I reminded myself of my strengths, and I recalled the extra hours of training I logged in my backyard in Rock City. My mind was a safe place to boast, *You deserve to be here Sally . . . no one wants this more than you . . .* My mind was a weapon. I had nothing to prove to anyone except myself.

When it was time for conditioning and Coach lined us up for sprints, I beat every girl to the other side of the field—it was my favorite way to end a training session and I prayed it would leave a lasting impression on the coach. At the end of practice and when every last player had left, I waited nervously to talk with the coach. He approached me with a smile and said, "You're a strong player Sally, and I think you'd be a great fit for the team. I understand you're looking for a scholarship and I'm more than happy to offer you one."

Shocked, I had to hold myself back from hugging him, "Coach, you have no idea how much this means to me! Thank you so much for this opportunity. I promise I will work hard! Thank you, thank you!"

Next, I needed to find a job. Having a job and making money gave me a sense I was making progress in my crumbling world. Working also gave me somewhere to be instead of sitting idle in our dark apartment. Dad worked hard to put a roof over our heads and food on the table, so I didn't ask him to pay for soccer cleats, clothes, or my gym membership when I could I pay for them myself. My family's financial stress rested on my shoulders like a ton of bricks. What if Dad continued to get sick or what if he couldn't find work? How would our family be affected as Mama's condition worsened? Bringing home my own paychecks made me feel helpful and in control, or maybe that's what I was looking for, something—anything—to control.

I filled out job applications for coffee houses, cafes, and anywhere that had a *Now Hiring* sign. I landed a job at Togo's, a sandwich shop a mile from home, and occasionally, I covered Mama's shifts in the nursery at church when she wasn't feeling well.

As summer came to a close, my older sister and I prepared to start her senior year and my junior year at Adison High School, ten minutes from home. When the first day of school arrived, we reluctantly packed our backpacks and made the drive across town. We blasted Counting Crows as we drove along, bantering about how we were going to be the only losers at school with no friends. We hadn't taken time to visit the school in advance to search for our classes. Frankly, we didn't care.

The first day of school was worse than I imagined it would be. I sat in the back row of every class and kept to myself. At lunch, I wandered through the sea of students looking for my sister and gave up after ten minutes. Thoughts of my friends back at Mesa Valley High School ached, so I found a spot in the sun behind a building and slid my back down the wall until I was sitting on the pavement. I envisioned my friends together, laughing and teasing each other at lunch. Staring up at the blue sky, I whispered, "I hate it here." Mama was getting treatment at the City of Hope hospital that day and I clenched my fists, thinking of her sad eyes. Undoubtedly, she was listening to a doctor give her more dismal news. Every week it was the same thing—she wasn't getting better.

The bell rang, and I trudged to my last class of the day. I normally cared about school, but not today. I pretended to listen as the teacher lectured in a monotone voice, but my mind wandered. Just as I did as a child, I turned off the world around me and envisioned myself in another place—a place that didn't feel so heavy—and I stayed there until the bell rang.

The next day, my sister and I were in a car accident while driving to school. No other cars were involved, but when my sister tried to correct the steering wheel after veering away from a wild driver, she hit the curb and broke the car's axle. We sat in disbelief as the tow truck drove away with the car she just purchased a week prior. The *only* reason we could attend Adison was because my sister drove us—now we were unsure how we would get to school each day. Dad picked us up from the side of the road and drove us home. He had some news to tell us.

The day continued to get worse. At the same time my sister and I were in the accident, the private high school across the street from our apartment, part of our church campus, called Mom and graciously offered us school scholarships. When Mom told us the news, I was horrified and protested, "I don't want to go to a private school, Mama! I like public school. Plus they don't even have a girls' soccer team!"

But Mama insisted. It was important to her that we see the blessing and be grateful for the opportunity to go to a school where the teachers cared extra about the students. The ease of walking across the street to and from school would help Mama, but I was tired of the constant changes. Sure, the chance to be at a private school free of charge was generous and there were loving people in the school's administration who were aware of my family's tough situation. They wanted to help, and maybe that's why I didn't want to go to *that* school. I was *very* prideful. Too prideful to see even in the midst of my struggles, there was good happening. It's easy to turn inward when we're hurting, to lose sight of the glimmer beckoning us to stay hopeful. It takes strength to see the light in the darkness, and that strength is already inside us—it's been there all along.

The thought of stepping on campus and people feeling sorry for me made me cringe. I also held harsh views about kids at private schools—they were spoiled, rich kids who didn't have to work for anything because everything was handed to them. I envisioned the worst situations about my first day attending a private school. Unaware at the time, my bitterness was intertwined with pain.

Pain

Controlled by pain,
Driven by shame,
We put others down.
Defending our hurt,
We stand in the dirt,
Wearing our pride,
Like a crown.

-yellowrunner

CHAPTER 15

SMILE

I didn't smile at the camera. From the moment I stepped onto the high school campus, I felt I didn't fit in, or maybe I didn't want to fit in. The harsh gymnasium lights lit up my face as the photographer asked, "Can you give us a little smile, Sally?" I mockingly turned one corner of my mouth up a half millimeter as the camera flash peered into my stormy eyes. That photo was placed on my eleventh grade ID card—a card I still carry around with me today. It serves as a reminder of the girl I once was—that girl who frequently weaves her bleeding heart into my writing. It's a physical reminder of how far I've come and overcome.

My older sister found me in the gymnasium and we scoffed at the sight of our faces on the blue and yellow plastic rectangle. Next to our photo was a circle with the words NOT VALID printed inside it, which meant we didn't pay the extra fee for the special blue sticker that would get us discounts on school activities and sporting events. Having the blue sticker made the ID card more valuable, and not having the sticker was a public announcement that you either couldn't afford the sticker or you had no interest in attending school functions—which led to further speculation about your social status. The space was a reminder of what I didn't have and the measures of value I recklessly tried to reach. My card wasn't valuable, and I smirked at the irony of the two words. If the battle within me had a title, there it was, printed in all capital letters next to my stoic face, SALLY-NOT VALID.

Before walking to my first class, I retreated to a nearby bathroom and sat in a stall to take a mental inventory. Quieting the hurt was becoming a necessary daily effort to exist in whatever environment I was in. Regularly, I fought to display who I was—who I believed I was. I wanted to trust the way Mama saw me, strong and joyful—but I questioned the validity of those two adjectives, and my questioning resulted from the sheer sight of Mama and her dwindling form. Was I being true to myself if I smiled while Mama coiled in pain at home? Was I lying to think of myself as strong when all I felt was weak?

Those who knew me, knew me outside the home when I was at my happiest. Suppressing sadness was easier than being vulnerable. Acutely aware of the difference between the odd or antisocial kids and the kids who were friendly and grinning, I leaned into the favorable mood. After all, how often do we speculate about the pleasant people in the school hallway?

Despite my initial judgmental attitude about private school kids, I made friends. The number of students who went out of their way to introduce themselves to me humbled me, especially Shannon, who remains to be one of the most loyal and kind friends I have ever known. Each morning, when I walked onto the school campus, the women who worked in the administrative office smiled and waved to me. It wasn't long before I understood that some ladies in the office had known me since I was a little girl because they were friends with Mama. One woman in particular was a special friend to Mama because she survived Stage 4 bone marrow cancer. Mama told me that if God could miraculously heal Shandra, then He could heal her, too.

I admired how Mama suffered yet remained hopeful of being healed. My faith felt weak compared to Mama's faith, and on those hard days, I tried to work on my faith by sneaking into the church sanctuary on the other side of campus. Like a child, I thought sitting in a church building meant I would be closer to God. I snuck away from the crowds during lunch break and with my journal tucked under my arm, I tiptoed through a giant wooden door in search of peace. I peered through the glass windows in the lobby to make sure no one was around, and then I creeped into the back row and folded my legs onto the pew. With a loud mind and thoughts that never stopped, I was drawn to the quiet.

In the sanctuary, I asked God to change my life, or at least give me a different one. Mama taught me to be honest with God because she said He already knew what I was going to pray before I spoke. And I asked God about that, too. Why should I pray if He already knew what I was going to say? If He knew my hurt and it never went away, did He not care? When sadness consumed me and my body ached, I slid onto the floor beneath the pews and soaked the carpet with my tears. The sanctuary, by its very definition, became my hiding place that year.

Because there was no soccer team for the girls, I told the coach I wanted to play on the boys' team. I told him I already had a few years' experience playing on a boy's soccer team and I didn't mind playing with them. Surprised by my offer but also without another option, the coach agreed to let me play on the team. When a few other girls found out, they asked to play, too. Pretty soon there were enough girls to form a team before the season started. I was happy to play a part in forming the team, but I was especially happy for my mom, knowing she could come watch a game or two, like she used to.

My club soccer team traveled frequently, and I either got a ride from the coach or drove myself. Since Mama wasn't doing well, it was rare for her to be on the sidelines. Not having Mom on the sidelines felt different. I was used to hearing her voice and anytime she cheered, I pushed a little harder. She never played soccer growing up, so she got excited whether we won or lost simply because spectating brought her joy.

I bought an annual pass to the local twenty-four-hour gym and after organizing my weekly schedule, I filled the hours after work with training sessions at the gym. My weekdays started around 6:30 a.m. and after school, I practiced with the high school soccer team. If I had club soccer practice, I trained with the high school team for one hour, then drove to club practice. After club practice, I worked the night shift at the sandwich shop. It was rare if I fell asleep before midnight most days of the week.

With so much independence, it was obvious I was growing up fast, and I navigated grown up situations on my own, like when my boss, at Togo's, made a spectacle of me at work one afternoon. He asked me to climb atop the giant ice machine and fix the vent, and while I was on display, he sneakily gestured to my coworkers to check out my ass. I turned around when I heard whispering and snickering and caught my boss gesturing sexually with a big smile on his face. When I looked at him, I nervously laughed it off—what else was I supposed to do? I kept these types of incidents to myself and filled the unstable spaces with whatever stability I could find. As the first semester of my junior year came to a close, I settled into a rhythm of school, soccer, work, gym, repeat.

CHAPTER 16

STANDING IN THE RAIN

It rained during the last soccer game of my junior year in high school. We were six weeks into 1996, and Mom's energy was noticeably and rapidly declining. Most of her days were spent balancing doctor appointments, kids' schedules, and relishing in any quality time she had with her family. Some days she had a bit of energy to complete a few tasks around the house, and other times the cancer or side effects of her treatments forced her to bed. My high school soccer season was ending, and we planned to play our last game on what turned out to be a gray, rainy day.

Historically, game day was the highlight of my week. My love for soccer and dream to one day become a professional athlete made game day that much more exciting—I lived for it! The days and nights before a game, I envisioned how the match would play out. I'd see the ball at my feet, running down the field, and then taking the perfect shot on goal. Each game brought me closer to my college goal and encouraged me to train a little harder.

I felt confused and partly guilty. How should I be acting? Should I be focusing on soccer and training while Mama's health crumbled at home? I hated envisioning the future without her encouraging voice speaking into my life. How could this be the plan for my future? I needed her here. She had always been there— cheering for me on the sidelines or welcoming my frustrated rants on the car ride home after a defeat. No one knew me like Mama and no one urged me to persevere more than her. Things would soon be different. I could feel it.

Would soccer eventually lose its effervescence? Maybe the greatest part about pursuing my dream was the fact she was on the journey with me. The actual goal paled compared to her presence. Her illness forced me to take a hard look at the substance of my dream. Did I love soccer as much as I thought I did? Maybe what I loved was making her proud, sharing stories, and hearing her call out to me as I ran up and down the field. All those moments, those days, those years—she was there. She made my dream feel alive.

The rain fell gently as our soccer team clamored onto the school bus for our last game of the season. Voices bounced across the seats and spontaneous singing filled the bus as we pulled from the driveway. Rain rarely fell in Southern California and when it did, we knew our soccer games were going to be more about the mud than anything else. I chatted with my good friend Kelly, and we laughed with each other about how terrible our footing was going to be in the slippery conditions. Anytime I was with my team, I felt better. Whether my teammates knew what was going on in my life or not, I loved being around them and knew at some point we'd be laughing together.

As we pulled into the parking lot, a few girls spotted their parents walking toward the field and shouted out the windows to get their attention. I watched the exchanges and smiled, partly envious. We crowded into the aisle as the bus came to a stop, laughing and shouting our way onto the pavement. Even though I knew my mom would not be sitting with the other parents, I gave way to my hopeful imagination and glanced at the sidelines. Hiding the reality of her absence from my last game was harder than I thought it would be, and my vivid imagination shoved an image of her into my mind—she was at home, alone, in pain.

I angrily curled my fingers into a fist and ran toward the bathroom. Happily, I shouted, "Gotta pee!" I let the image of her linger for a few seconds as I ran along. I visualized a few strands of her remaining dark hair beneath her bandana. I hated that she had to lose her hair for a second time—it was a cruel side effect to her already insurmountable suffering. I neared the bathroom door just as a teammate popped out and immediately, the picture of Mama vanished.

I threw my teammate a wide grin and put up my hand for a high-five, saying, "You ready to play in some mud!"

She gave me a high-five back, "Heck yeah!" I continued inside the bathroom, pausing to survey my face in the mirror. I made sure no tears had escaped and after a few deep breaths, joined my team on the field.

During the second half, the rain started up again, soaking our hair and thick soccer socks. The mud at center field formed a slippery pit, and we hollered in our vain attempts to dribble through it. I sloppily maneuvered around the last defender in a breakaway down the field. Thirty yards and a goalie were my only concern. As I neared the goal, I glanced up to place my shot, but was immediately gripped by a figure in the corner of the field. It was her, standing beneath a gray umbrella, wearing her favorite blue jacket. Her sunken eyes against her pale skin pulled at me just as I clumsily released a shot that went sailing over the crossbar. "Mama! What are you doing?" I sprinted to her as the goalie ran behind the goal to retrieve the ball.

As if standing tall would make her appear stronger, Mama straightened herself up and smiled with her whole body, "Oh, I just wanted to see you play." I was slightly shorter than her and when we hugged, my face met the short brown wig styled into a bob haircut, reminding me that Mama's body wasn't strong— it was sick. I grieved at the whiff of her artificial hair and the sadness I knew it brought her. I was missing things about Mama I never noticed I loved so much before. The details that uniquely made up who she was from the way she walked to the way she threw her head back when she laughed—all these things were washing away before me.

I tightly hugged her, "Thank you for being here Mama. I can't believe you're here . . . are you okay?"

She brushed off my concern with a cheery tone, "You know I love watching you play. You're doing great!"

I grabbed her hand and squeezed it, "I love you." Her fingers oddly felt smaller than mine, and her skin was cold. I knew if I stayed any longer, I would cry and look weak—at least that's how my sixteen-year-old mind understood weakness.

Weakness was tears and crying and cowering in a heap on the floor. Weakness was letting others see my feelings. Weakness was the entryway to failure and everything I worked so hard to overcome. I didn't want to be weak.

But there was something I didn't know at the time. Mama knew I was hiding my tears, and she later told me the concern it brought her. Mama knew me better than I thought, and she understood I mustered up a hardness for so long it became the armor I chose to wear. I thought I was fooling her, but she was more than aware.

The referee blew his whistle for a goal kick—perfect timing. I turned and ran down the line, spinning my body just as they kicked the ball. I secretly glanced back at Mama, catching the smile on her face despite the rain that had just begun to fall in full force. I knew her eyes were watching me play for what I vainly hoped wouldn't be the last time.

Transfixed on the picture of her standing there, an image that is forever branded in my mind, I remember the wrestling of love and hardness within me. Rebellious tears escaped down my cheeks and I was thankful for the rain right then because no one could tell the difference between raindrops and tears.

I don't recall whether or not we won that game, and it doesn't matter. But I do remember Mama. I think we'll always remember people more than win. When I hit a low point in a race or when life gets difficult, sometimes I think back to this day:

Stand in the Rain

I remember Mama standing in the rain
And how she was okay not having muscles to display.
I remember running to her on the field that day.
I remember being wet and uncomfortable as we embraced,
And her loving smile despite the path she faced.
And even though she was sick, she didn't complain.
Because Mama wanted to show me, we
can choose strength in pain.
She knew strength is a choice, not a look or a feeling.
Mama chose strong because that's what happens
when strength is rooted in love:
We endure a little more;
We hope a little more.
And when the whole world focuses on a superficial frame,
We can choose to be strong and stand in the rain.

-yellowrunner

CHAPTER 17

WHEELCHAIR

A few weeks after the rainy high school soccer game, I found Mama in a wheelchair. I came home from a weekend soccer tournament with my club team and when I walked through the front door, there she was, sunken eyes, staring back at me. I dropped my bag in the middle of the kitchen and hurried to her side, shocked that after only a couple of days, she went from walking to being confined to a chair. I vainly asked questions about what happened and how she was feeling, hopeful she would shock me and say the chair was a temporary pit stop on her road to recovery. At this point in Mama's illness, it was becoming more common to feel lame and disappointed by my own questions, yet I persisted because I believed my questioning let her know how much I cared. Somewhere in my questioning, a little girl still existed, longing for her Mama to say, "I'm going to be okay, and so are you."

Unlike my peers, I was being schooled in a subject I didn't sign up for. The subject was called Death 101 and my teacher was nowhere to be found. I learned to navigate the crumbling ground beneath me alone. At times, I felt like I was clawing at the walls, panicking for something to hold on to, begging for the floor to stop from breaking away beneath me. I toiled over my work and training schedule, contemplating if I should stay home more. Being in Mama's presence was simultaneously the only place I wanted to be—and pure hell.

For years, I witnessed the monster hurt my family, and sometimes, I was forced to watch the affliction up close, anxiously waiting for it to end. Now cancer was mercilessly tormenting Mama and I couldn't save her from it. I couldn't stand up to cancer for Mama the same way I stood up to the monster. This cancer was cruel and unrelenting, daily sucking the light from her beautiful brown eyes.

The cancer moved into her bone marrow, around her brain, and into her abdomen. She was in constant pain, and the only relief she found was in the multiple pills doctors prescribed her. Those pills made her hallucinate and when I sat quietly by her side, sometimes she looked at me in horror and yelled, "I'm in hell! I'm in hell! Why are you just sitting there? Why don't you help me? HELP ME!"

Her episodes startled me and I tried explaining I was right there with her but it seldom helped, only making the turmoil worse. I was losing her, and I was helpless amid her torture. Mama thought we were all watching from afar as she suffered, and I didn't know how to comfort her. By this time, I accepted her diagnosis and told myself there was no healing to come. I spent most nights talking to God, wrestling with sleep and nightmares of her leaving. I begged God to take Mama home instead of dragging her through misery. If she was going to die, why did death have to last this long? Why couldn't she die in peace?

On nights I couldn't sleep, I tiptoed from my bedroom and down the dark hallway to check on Mama. Nurses put a hospital bed in our living room. It sat cold and imposing in the center of the room, and I was filled with dread by its symbolism of death. It was a stale, emotionless object that seemed to revel in the discomfort it brought to those forced to lay on it.

The bed reminded me of the hospital—a place I loathed. At sixteen years old, my only encounters with the hospital stemmed from death and sadness—tearfully saying goodbye to people I loved, visiting those in discomfort, and battling the ever present feeling that once we passed through the hospital doors, we were no longer humans with feelings and thoughts, rather just numbers. Patient #238—Breast Cancer, Stage IV, Terminal.

Mama didn't always take large doses of pills. One night, she just lay in my lap and asked me to massage her head because the agony inside was unbearable. Oddly, I felt honored she asked me to ease her pain. I carefully set my ten fingers around her hairless skull and gently massaged into the bandana covering it. She closed her eyes, and I whispered a song over her as tears streamed down her sunken cheeks. With her in my lap, I reminisced about the times she cared for me when I was sick. Times when I curled up on the couch beneath a blanket, and she scratched my back or gently played with my hair to help me fall asleep. She was always there, waiting to tend to me. And now, the tables had turned. With her on the couch and me intent on easing her discomfort, I leaned toward her ear and thanked her for all the times she cared for me.

As Mama's condition worsened, she needed our help with the most basic needs. She knew she was getting weaker, but she didn't want to admit it. One afternoon, while I was in my room, she called out to me. Upon entering her bedroom, I caught her trying to push her wheelchair over the threshold that separated her bathroom from the bedroom. The wheels hit the divider and her frail arms couldn't push over it. I stepped behind her chair and gently nudged it forward, just as she let out a big sigh. She said nothing, but I noted the sweat on her forehead.

"Mama, how long have you been trying to do this?"

Frustrated, she responded, "I just want to go to the bathroom by myself."

At sixteen, I didn't understand what it felt like to call upon my child to help me go to the bathroom. I'm sure Mama never expected that day to come—or at least, not so quickly.

I moved to the front of her wheelchair and lowered into a deep squat position, and when her sad eyes met mine, I told her to wrap her arms around my neck. "I'm gonna lift you on the count of three, okay?"

Mama gave a faint nod and lifted her willowy arms to embrace my neck. Then fearfully blurted out, "You better not drop me, Sally."

I responded assertively, "You know I'm strong. I got you."

If there was anything I knew to do well, it was lift. I knew to keep my back straight and to contract my abs as I wrapped my arms tightly around her torso. I shoved my toes beneath the wheels so the chair wouldn't move, and then pulled her toward me. She grunted in discomfort. With a deep breath and a, "One, two, three!" I lifted her from the chair. For a split second, I wavered—lifting a limp body differed from lifting a barbell, and sweat beaded on my forehead as I feigned confidence. With a heave and an awkward pivot, I set her on the toilet.

She was briefly quiet and kept her head down. Then, clearly defeated, she lifted her head and whispered, "I need to pull down my pants."

And with that one request, she cried. I clenched my jaw at the sight of her tears in an attempt to hide my sadness, "It's okay, Mama, I should have done that first. No big deal."

My words felt weak as I helped her.

I wanted to take her sadness away with my words.
I wanted to comfort her anguish with hope for the future.
I wanted to tell her she was going to be okay.
But, I couldn't look at her and lie.
Because the truth was, she would never be okay again.
She was getting worse with each passing day.
This.
This is what dying looked like.

LIFT, PULL, CARRY

I started lifting when I was sixteen.
I lifted at night after work.
I didn't have a training partner.
It was just me and the clock,
Just me and the mirror.
I'd look at my body and the men throwing iron next to me;
It motivated me.
I didn't care I was usually the only girl grabbing dumbbells.
I didn't care that sometimes I was the
only one in the gym at night.
I had a dream;
I had rage;
I had sadness.
I was lonely, but you'd never know it.
Because who felt what I felt?
Who hurt like me?
No one knew because I kept it all in.
I was tough and numb and had a bigger smile than anyone.
Sometimes I thought,
Maybe all this pain is gonna mean something.
Maybe all this work will pay off.
Maybe.
So I lifted,
Month after month,
Year after year.
Lift, Pull, Carry,
The body I have today didn't form overnight.
I didn't lift because strength training was popular.
I didn't lift to accent a body part,
No.
I lifted to be strong.
I lifted to endure the pain.
I lifted because I didn't believe I had worth,

But I did believe I could work
as hard as anyone.
And when I finally achieved a dream,
They questioned my lifting.
They scoffed at my training.
And it stung.
I'm human.
I questioned myself, too.
But I kept lifting,
Because that's how Mama raised me:
Lift others up.
Pull for those who are weary.
Carry kindness wherever you go.
Lift, Pull, Carry.
I'm not always good at doing those things.
I've had seasons of weakness.
I'm still learning and
building this one body given to me.
This poem is for you, my friend,
I see you.
You're not alone.
I promise, there *are* people
who feel what you feel,
even if it's just me.
These words are for weary hearts burning
the midnight oil in pursuit of a dream.
It feels lonely sometimes;
But you're not alone.
Keep going.
It *is* worth it,
even if you can't see it yet.
Lift,
Pull,
Carry.

-yellowrunner

135

CHAPTER 18

YELLOWRUNNER

My seventeenth birthday is forever etched in my memory—a beautiful spring day on April 30, 1996. Every year on my birthday, I remember the story I'm about to share with you, the start of the hardest season of my life. This memory is painted yellow in my mind and it's how my pen and profile name, *yellowrunner* came about. When I first began using Instagram, I chose @yellowrunner for my profile. For over a decade, people have thought I chose that nickname because I like the color yellow, which I do, but that's not the reason for the name. ***Yellowrunner*** *is a message of strength and hope—to keep moving forward no matter the circumstance.* If you've ever glanced at the symbolism of colors, something I've had fun doing over the years, you'll find the color yellow holds several meanings, but the symbol that sticks out to me the most is *hope*. Yellow is often associated with light, and I believe every person who lives bears a unique light. To shine your light is to live courageously and I've always wanted my running to bear that message. No matter where we are in our journey, we need to know and believe that we *are* strong and that we *are* capable of enduring every step in our unique story. I hope whenever you see the color yellow, you'll be reminded of the strength inside you too.

On my birthday, I found myself seated at the foot of Mama's wheelchair, gazing up at her. She breathed heavily, exhausted from her trip to the store with Dad. Only an hour prior, I stood pleading with Mama from the entryway, "You don't have to do this. Please, I know you're tired." But Dad was already lifting her withered frame from the wheelchair into the car. Mama met my worried gaze and said reassuringly, "I'm okay, Sally. I really want to do this."

Mama made up her mind. She was going to the store. I squeezed my fists into the pockets of my overalls and watched our maroon 1969 Ford Fairmont wagon pull from the driveway. Dad's focused expression made me uneasy. Was he feeling like me? How would the scene play out once Dad and Mom arrived at the store? How long would they stay there? What if people stared at Mama as Dad wheeled her up and down the aisles? Her bald head and emaciated body would surely cause people to turn their heads. I didn't want people judging her frailty—they didn't know how strong she was. She was the strongest person I had ever known, but to the outside world, she was a gaunt image of sickness. Why did I care so much about how others saw her? When I looked at her, I saw *my* Mama, beautiful and strong—the same woman I had known since day one.

Now she was back home, weary and clenching a shopping bag across her lap like a trophy. Mama needed to go to the store because not only would it be the last time she bought someone a gift, but it would be the last time she celebrated a birthday, *mine*.

Birthdays were a big deal in our home—no matter our financial situation. Mama made sure each of her children felt extra special on their big day. Each year, she baked cakes with sprinkles on top. If it was your birthday, you got to lick the cake batter from the bowl and pick out your very own box of Circus

Animal cookies, or Cheez-It crackers from the grocery store. The night before, Mama hung signs on the walls and scattered colorful balloons across the living room floor. Waking up on your birthday morning was the most exciting day of the year.

This birthday, however, was a stark contrast to past celebrations and a nagging ache spread throughout my body, dulling the anticipation I typically experienced with each passing year. I stared at the bag in Mama's lap instead of her face because I knew if I looked at her, I would surrender years of locked up emotions. She shifted in her wheelchair and gathered herself to sit a little taller. She had something important to say, "Sally, look at me . . ." She paused as I drew in a deep breath and looked up, woefully scanning her face. A tsunami of tears pulsated behind my eyes, and as she spoke, I released them at her feet.

"Happy Birthday to my Little Bear. You know I love you so much and I am so proud of who you are becoming . . ."

But I frantically interrupted, "Mama wait . . ." overcome by the realization of what was really happening, I grabbed her hand and stared at the carpet in an attempt to gather myself and then looked back at her.

She continued speaking, "You are strong, Sally, and I have always been so proud to be your Mama. You are my Sunshine . . ." And then from the bags, she pulled out a yellow picture frame, a yellow clock, and a yellow candle.

I took each gift as her thin hands set them into mine. "I love them . . . thank you." Keeping my face down, I set the presents on the carpet and awkwardly wiped away the tears that wouldn't go away.

I felt her eyes on me as she continued, "Sally, I wish I could stay here with you. I know it's going to be hard sometimes when I'm gone, but I don't want you to turn bitter. Keep being Sally—keep shining bright in all you do . . ."

I interrupted her again and with a tear soaked shirt, rose onto my knees, gently draping myself onto her bony legs. I didn't want to hear what sounded like saying goodbye. It felt like I was watching the ending scene in a really sad movie, and movies weren't real. This whole interaction didn't feel real.

"No, Mama, please!" Wrapping my arms around her, I protested, "I don't feel strong . . . I'm not strong." I didn't know what to say. What words are formed by a child grasping for understanding at a time such as this? I resorted to saying the only meaningful thing I knew to say, "I love you Mama." The love I felt for Mama was intense in that moment and maybe if I repeated those three words, everything I thought and felt about her would be understood. The overflowing, abundant power of love didn't need other words.

"You *are* strong, Sally, you have always been strong." Mama lovingly touched the back of my head as I wept in her lap. She whispered, "You're gonna be okay."

I anxiously leaned back onto the carpet and fumbled with the gifts, noting each one was yellow, like the color of the sun. I stared at them for a minute, and a lonely shiver gripped me with such intensity, I shook. Just as a frightened child buries into their mother, I instinctively buried myself back into Mama.

We wept together. I can only imagine now that she must have had a million things she wanted to say—a mother's last message to her daughter.

A desperation rose in me and I lifted my head to search her face for comfort, "I don't want you to go Mama . . . I don't want you to go . . ."

Over and over again,
That's all I could say.
From the mouth of a child
In the arms of her mother,
"Please, don't go."

CHAPTER 19

THIS IS PERMANENT

On May twenty-eighth, he swung at me above Mama's body. Abruptly, he told my four siblings and me to leave the living room where Mama was obviously taking her last breaths. My siblings obeyed, but I stayed. Why would I leave her side? Just two weeks prior, the monster became agitated with Mama after she yelped in pain as he attempted to change her diaper. She weakly asked him to be careful, but instead he became angry and punished her by leaving her exposed for all to see in the living room. One of my sisters quickly tended to her and finished changing her. I was working the night it happened and was furious when I later heard about it, so when the monster told us to leave the room, I refused.

The monster glared at me from the other side of her bed and threatened to hurt me if I didn't do as he commanded, but I glared back at him, unafraid. "I'm staying."

I looked down at Mama and touched her cheek, "I'm right here." A Bible was by her side and I opened it to the book of Psalms and began reading to her. Without hesitation, the monster snarled and swung at me above Mom's face. I leaned back and Mama's hands shot straight in the air as if to protect me. Her eyes were the size of golf balls and she let out a moan and then her arms dropped like logs back onto the bed. Rage welled inside me and he snarled again, demanding I leave. Mama's breath rattled as she struggled to breathe. Reluctantly, I left her side, the image of violence was in no way the picture Mama deserved in her last moments on earth.

Mama clung to life for an additional day, as if to make sure her children were okay. As we gathered around her bedside on May 29, 1996, tears streaming down our faces, I fixated on the rise and fall of her chest. Despite my attempts to prepare myself for this moment, the reality of her leaving hit me with a force I could never have imagined. As I sat at her feet, I felt a part of me dying with her.

Earlier that week, Mama managed to mumble her favorite Bible verse which is also inscribed on her tombstone, Jeremiah 29:11, "For I know the thoughts that I think toward you, says the Lord, thoughts of peace and not of evil, to give you a future and a hope" (NKJV). She desperately wanted her children to continue in life, knowing that a future and hope awaited us. But I wasn't thinking of my future as she drifted away. I couldn't imagine a future without her.

The room felt noticeably colder, and my eyes darted around the bed, taking in the shattered faces of my family. Our hands rested on Mama, simultaneously offering her comfort and secretly hoping by some great power our clinging would keep her with us a little longer. All at once, darkness rushed in and her body rose and fell one last time. Her face slowly froze, and…she was gone.

We stayed still, tormented by the undeniable truth that comes with the first moments of death. *This is permanent.* One by one, we waited to spend a final moment with Mama. When it was my turn, raw fear welled inside me. As I stepped toward her, I reached to touch her cheek. It was frighteningly cold, and when I bent toward her ear, the absence of her breath screamed into my face like a pack of hyenas, "SHE'S NOT THERE! SHE CAN'T HEAR YOU! SHE'S GONE!" I grabbed onto the stale metal bed railing and took a step away from her. She was right there, or was she? I couldn't hear my own words as they came from my mouth. Her death was too loud. I stood, entranced by her petrified corpse, when all of a sudden, fear grabbed me by the throat and squeezed so tightly I choked, gagging on my tears. *What the hell is going on?* I moved away from the figure I used to call Mama and suddenly felt myself watching *Me* from the other side of the room. *This isn't real . . . this isn't real.*

Like a zombie, I shuffled down the hallway. What are you supposed to do immediately after your Mom dies? Does anyone know the answer? I still don't know. I don't recall us coming together for comfort in those hours—only the quiet, muffled cries of my siblings as they wept in solitude.

A knock at the front door made me jump, and then the sound of unfamiliar voices and steps entered our home. I anxiously walked to the living room where two strangers stood surveying Mom. Within minutes, they covered her body and wheeled her metal bed through the kitchen and out the front door. I followed, pausing to watch from the porch. The strange humans stopped behind an ugly, awkwardly shaped vehicle and then pushed her bed into full view. Seeing her frame draped in a white sheet made me panic. My mind raced, thinking about the chance that maybe she wasn't dead and maybe she had only fallen asleep. I obsessed over the thought as they lifted her into the car,

What if she wakes up?!

Wait!

She's *not* dead!

God wouldn't *really* take her;
He knows I *need* her.
Stop!

But I couldn't move. I couldn't speak. I stood motionless in my silent turmoil, paralyzed by the nightmare that wasn't a nightmare at all. It was reality.

I watched the strange vehicle pull from the curb, and then stared as it disappeared from my view. My eyes shifted to the fully grown willow tree in our front lawn. A white wooden swing hung from a branch. That swing was the last place I sat with Mama for a picture. She loved that tree and the way the branches hung like a canopy all around us. Staring for a minute more, I suddenly felt the coldness of the metal screen door in my hand. I didn't want to go in the house, and I hesitated for a moment before stepping inside and closing the front door. It felt strange closing the door knowing Mama was on the outside—she'd never come through the front door again.

Back in my room, all I wanted to do was bury myself in blankets and be left alone. Before getting into bed, I grabbed my Bible from the dresser. It was the only thing that made me feel close to Mama. So many times I saw her sit peacefully with her Bible, and I wanted that peace, too. I closed my eyes, and whispered to God, "I know she's with You. Why can't I be there, too?" A dismal feeling swept over me as I continued, "I don't even know what to read. Give me something, please." I am not one for superstition or seeing God as a genie, but when I opened my Bible, I aimlessly flipped to the book of Psalms and randomly settled onto Chapter 46. One verse jumped off the page, "Be still and know that I am God;" (Psalm 46:10 NKJV). I sighed and promptly shut the book. How do I do that? I had heard the verse many times before and negatively whispered to myself, "Of course that's the verse I turn to."

Being still was . . . and still is, a difficult thing for me, but *maybe* those words were what I needed in that moment. Later on, I learned the Hebrew meaning for "be still" is [1]"to let go, to release" and it moved me to tears. I didn't want to let go of Mama. It would take time for me to understand the power and healing of letting go of the things I couldn't control. I don't understand why there's so much pain and suffering in the world; and I don't understand why some people suffer more than others, but I do know even in the midst of so much hurt, Hope exists.

Letting go of Mama and moving forward with my life was going to be a painfully slow climb to the top of the Mountain. One day, I would discover that this climb would be where I'd gain the greatest strength— letting go and holding onto Hope.

I shut off the light and pulled my blankets to my face; images from the night appeared in my mind and I obsessed over every one:

Me at Mama's feet,

The heave of her last breath,

The lighting in the room,

The darkness inside,

And her body covered up, as they took her far, far away.

---

[1] https://lp.israelbiblicalstudies.com/lp_iibs_biblical_hebrew_let_go-en. html?cid=68184&adgroupid=-1&utm_source=Community&utm_medium=FB_insights&utm_campaign=BIB_EN_COM_FB_Let_Go_2019-03-20_68184&commChannel=1

HOPE

Take my hand,
as darkness closes in;
and hope with me.
No need to smile or pretend;
your tears,
are precious to me.
The light is far,
from where we stand;
but there's a glimmer,
around the bend.
Hope with me.
Hope with me.
Hope.

-yellowrunner

CHAPTER 20

BROKEN

Within a couple weeks of burying Mama, Dad was diagnosed with a massive brain tumor. They found the tumor on his pituitary gland and estimated it had been there for almost a decade, which was roughly how long they assumed Mama had cancer. They were both sick at the same time, and since our family didn't have health insurance until Mama started receiving government aid, all focus had been on her, not Dad.

Between his sick wife, losing our home, and a business with continual ups and downs, Dad's stress levels were off the charts. What they originally thought were migraines were actually acromegaly, a very rare but serious condition that produces high levels of growth hormone. Dad's tumor was benign (noncancerous) but was still life threatening because of its location in his brain. Acromegaly is a form of gigantism, and had Dad still been in his youth, it would have caused his bones to grow to an abnormal size. Because he was already a full-grown adult, it mainly affected his tissues, hands, and feet. He had to cut his wedding ring off his now giant hand and buy special size shoes for his expanding feet. His teeth slowly separated and his head and body swelled in unusual ways. His daily migraines were excruciating and since only a handful of people per million get acromegaly, doctors scrambled with how to treat him.

Dad's diagnosis startled our diluted family and to some extent, felt like a sick joke. Still trying to mourn the loss of Mama, I wondered if God was going to take Dad, too. My older sister graduated from high school a week after Mama's funeral and then promptly packed up her bedroom. With longing, I watched her shove piles of clothes and shoes into the back of her car. Only thirteen months apart, we were naturally close to each other and as she drove away, I felt a pang of sadness. Oh, how I wished I could be in the passenger seat next to her.

With a year of high school remaining, I promised Mama I would look after my little sisters while the three of us went to school together. Now, with only four of us left in the house, the environment changed. The house was quieter and meals were lonelier, so I did my best to stay busy. Knowing I needed to drive back home at some point during the day filled me with dread. I couldn't escape walking into the place where Mama died.

Suffocating grief stayed with me throughout every day, but I did my best to hide it. I didn't want to be treated differently because Mama died. I didn't want people to feel sorry for me, and it felt awkward when well-meaning friends tried their best to come up with a comforting word to say to me.

As the months passed, my nightly prayer filled the darkness with desperate requests for God to kill me. I obsessed over the idea of dying and the undeniable relief it would bring to my harassed mind. Sometimes, I shamefully buried my face into my pillow contemplating the difference between accidental death and suicide. I witnessed the aftermath of suicide more than once in my life and the intense grief and suffering it brought on those left behind rippled through my mind. What if I accidentally fell off the freeway bridge, which was just a stone's throw from my front door? What if I walked into the ocean and accidentally drowned? My own thoughts horrified me—I had never been so low.

All my life I prided myself in being able to overcome difficulties with my mind. But now, a new monster lurked, and this monster broke into the depths of me. This monster taunted me with lies that without Mama, I wasn't as strong as I thought I was. The monster crept into the quiet moments of my day when I tried to study or sleep, and he heckled me with constant reminders of her absence.

Every night, I was tormented by the same dream about Mama. At first, it appeared to be a joyful reunion as I ran toward her with a smile on my face. However, the closer I got, the more confused I became by the frozen expression on her face. Just as I reached out to embrace her, she dissolved into a cloud of dust. The scene was then swallowed by a fierce storm and the entire atmosphere came crashing down on top of me. This nightmare repeated itself night after night, leaving me in tears and trembling with fear as I woke in the dead of night.

My sad thoughts consumed me, and I tried my best to resist their control over me. Mama promised the road ahead would be difficult, but she encouraged me to hold fast to my faith and hope for better days ahead. Contemplating her words, I wondered if believing her encouragement would help me. What if she was wrong? The only way to find out was to keep moving forward.

I picked up another job as a hostess at a local diner and then left my position at Togo's to become a barista at Muddy's Coffee House. Working five to six days a week and then training at the gym into the late hours of the night was the healthiest coping mechanism my adolescent brain could find. Dad didn't like my routine and harshly told me that I was selfish and not part of the family. Without access to a therapist and no basic knowledge how to process the loss of a parent, I believed working and training was a far better option than doing drugs or binging on alcohol. No doubt, there were countless other unhealthy ways for me to cope. Being at home made my whole body ache. *Why couldn't Dad understand I was hurting too?*

Dad was scheduled to have brain surgery just as summer break began. The intense pain he experienced made it difficult to fulfill his work obligations, and every day he desperately shook aspirin into his hand in a futile attempt to relieve his suffering. The thought of a surgeon performing a procedure on his brain seemed daunting, and the very phrase "brain surgery" instilled fear in me. As the days went by, I became more and more pessimistic about the outcome. It was difficult to keep the faith that my dad would recover.

The day of dad's brain surgery finally arrived, and I was tasked with picking him up from the hospital so the nurses could spend a few minutes teaching me how to care for him after his operation. I felt overwhelmed and alone, tears streaming down my face as I navigated the busy freeway to the hospital. I prayed as I drove. Filled with confusion and desperation, I questioned how this could happen to Dad so soon after losing Mama.

I pulled into a parking spot and turned off the engine. This was the first time I drove to the hospital alone. I clenched the steering wheel and stared toward the entrance, hating that I had to be the one to pick up Dad. I believe we should forgive others no matter what, but I struggled with forgiving someone who wasn't sorry. Dad held no remorse nor regret for the way he treated me over the years. If anything, he felt justified in his actions, continually reminding me of the reasons I deserved his punishments.

I'll be the first to say I wasn't a perfect child, but I did *try* to be perfect. Driven by hurt and my belief that who I was as a person was *not* enough, I considered every word Dad said to me. I often sat in my room after arguing with Dad and talked harshly to myself. As if Dad's words didn't hurt enough, I wrestled with whether or not he was right.

Most of the time I assumed he was right on the basis of faith. I was to be a respectful, obedient child, and my shortcomings reminded me that I was not only displeasing to Dad, but to God. Growing up, the pastors in church referred to God as "Our Father in Heaven," which led me to believe God was just as disappointed in me as my father on earth. This is why Mama's faith was so intriguing to me. She spoke about a God who was gracious, unconditionally loving, and who never changed His love for me regardless of how terrible or wonderful I behaved. Mama made me believe I could proudly stand on my own two feet, *unaltered and fully valid* in who I was meant to be. With her absence, I battled to keep her words louder in my mind than Dad's words.

I didn't know how to define my relationship with Dad. Occasionally, we had conversations, often led by one of my empty achievements. He confused me. Dad didn't know me, and the chasm that had been driven between us felt deeper with each passing year. He didn't *see* me. He only saw a child who disappointed him, and his bitter perspective of me never ceased to appear. We could go days, even weeks, having civil interactions, but he kept me on edge. It was only a matter of time before he rejected me, threatened me, or accused me of some outlandish wrongdoing.

The continual back and forth rocked my trust in him so deeply it started to affect the way I viewed and interacted with my other relationships. At times, I wondered if he knew I needed a dad—a father who loved me, all of me, no matter my mistakes or shortcomings. I asked God to help me forgive him because I didn't know how. I wanted to see him the way God saw him because when I looked at Dad, I saw hurt.

Dad was waiting for me, and I shuddered to think how he might look. The last time Mama was in the hospital before she died was the last time I ever wanted to set foot in a hospital again. Back and forth I stared at my watch and the entrance, remembering Mama's broken body and fearing Dad would be broken, too.

Once inside the hospital, I was directed to a door down the hall. My eyes darted left and right and my hands sweat as I caught glimpses of patients struggling in their beds. I crept toward the room where Dad was waiting and peered through the slender window in the door before opening it. I froze, catching a glimpse of his strangely large body slumped to one side of his wheelchair. Why was he in a wheelchair? My eyes fixated on his giant paw-like hand dangling slightly above the ground. His large head was shaved across the middle, from ear to ear, and a white bandage covered two mysterious, pointy shapes on the top of his head. The sight of blood oozing through the bandages made my stomach turn, and I hesitated to touch the door handle.

Dad looked like he just lost a gruesome battle and for the first time in a long time, I had compassion for him. I let my mind ease into grace as I envisioned what Dad must be feeling inside. Only a couple months prior, he lost his wife of over twenty years and before he could take his next breath, he was diagnosed with a rare and life-threatening brain tumor. I imagined the emotional pain he felt every moment of every day and tried to understand the depth of his physical pain. I couldn't even look at his bandages without feeling nauseous. What did the doctors do to him?

Drawing in a deep breath, I opened the door and timidly took one step into the bright room and then panicked—Dad looked dead. Wild thoughts screamed into my mind at the speed of light. *Is he dead? Why isn't he moving? Is he breathing? I don't think he's breathing!*

Suddenly, I was snapped from my trance when the nurse cheerily asked, "Hello there, are you Sally? Good to see you sweetie. Step over here and I'll show you how to tend to his bandages and give him a shot."

Frozen, I stared back at her, wondering if I was listening to a foreign language. I then shifted my eyes back to the wheelchair. I couldn't take my eyes off Dad's head. Speaking nonchalantly about shots and bandages, the nurse continued as if explaining how to make a peanut butter sandwich. Needles made me especially anxious and as the nurse fluttered between Dad's wheelchair and the table where she had gathered a few shots to practice with, I cautiously stepped to the front of Dad's body. His eyes were closed and his mouth was slightly open. At this moment, the nurse must have realized I wasn't okay and she slowed down next to me and quietly said, "Why don't I first show you what the surgeon did to your dad's head."

Dad's condition was so rare, doctors had traveled from afar just to examine him. They gathered together to discuss the best way to treat him, and discovered if they attempted to remove the entire tumor, they would kill him. So they removed as much of the tumor as they could, and then placed two giant metal bolts halfway into the top of his head. These bolts needed to stay partially exposed, so the skin wasn't allowed to heal together. The skin needed to be pulled away from the metal bolts each day and the bandages needed to be cleaned. The nurse explained that Dad would go to the hospital for several weeks in a row where doctors would hook his head up to a massive machine and attempt to radiate the rest of the tumor away. Once the treatment was complete, the doctors planned to remove the bolts from Dad's head. It was a new and risky treatment, but they assured Dad he was in good hands and this was his best option.

I had never seen a person with bolts in their head, and to this day, I still have never seen or heard of anyone having this procedure. To a child, it was a disgusting solution, and I imagined the excruciating pain it was causing Dad.

I studied Dad in his wheelchair, broken and weak.

I'm not sure if he remembers that day—they drugged him up pretty well.

But I like to think he remembers me being there for him.

I like to think that for that one day in my life,

We needed each other.

Like Daddy, I was broken.

He was human, like me—imperfect and in need.

In need of love and grace,

In need of healing and restoration,

In need of hope for better days.

I saw myself in Daddy that day,

Even if he doesn't remember.

I'll never forget that day because it was the day I started forgiving Dad. I say "started" because it took a lot of tries and a lot of years to forgive him. One of the most valuable things I continue learning in life is we can never forgive someone too much, no matter the offense. And I understand that might sound crazy, especially to those who have been deeply wronged.

I *see* you.

Forgiveness is the beginning of freedom, and even though I didn't know it at the time, freedom was what I longed for.

To be free from pain,

To be free from shame,

To be free from self-hatred,

I just wanted to be free.

CHAPTER 21

CHOOSE STRONG

Dad was arrested at school in front of my friends. It was six months between the day I picked him up from the hospital and the night he kicked my sister in the face. I was at work when it happened. When my sister confided in the school's Dean of Women about the obvious bruise on her face, she didn't know they would reveal her secret to the police. This single day in my story proved to be one of the most crushing days of my life—which feels overwhelming to say because Mama died only eleven months prior. With one dreadful event after another since her passing, I reached the *lowest point* in my journey.

Within that same time frame, I had begun my Senior year in high school and within a few weeks of school starting, I defeatedly watched my club soccer team dissolve. As the youngest member, I was left behind when my teammates started college. And despite the letters of interest from colleges across the country, I wrestled with the idea of continuing to pursue my soccer goals. The letters from coaches piled up on my bedroom dresser; several were from the colleges I had only dreamed about, but I felt lost. This wasn't how I had envisioned my life unfolding. Most days I didn't feel like playing soccer anymore; frankly, I didn't feel like doing anything at all. I had to force myself to go through the motions of each day; and as I moved through the hours, I punished myself with unanswerable questions. *Was it selfish to go away for college? Did soccer still hold the same value in my life?* It was the first time I questioned the whole meaning of sports. Maybe these were the natural questions that come when losing someone; we question what really matters in life. At the end of Mama's life, she couldn't take anything with her- no medals, no possessions. Death was a naked, lonely journey; and death had made Mama and all who witnessed her dying, question the purpose of life. One thing I knew to be true after she left, was that I didn't miss hearing about her accolades or the possessions she once owned, I missed *her*. I missed the way she made me feel when I was in her presence. I missed her hugs and the comfort I found at the sight of her smile. I missed our talks on the back porch beneath the stars back in Rock City; and I missed her quirky sense of humor and the way it made me belly laugh. *Who* Mama was outshined any accomplishment or material thing she owned.

Soccer was my one chance at going to college, but was soccer enough to make my one life meaningful? If my soccer career ended after college what did I have left? Who was I apart from soccer and the years of training I had devoted to it? With Mama gone and my older siblings living out of the house, I contemplated what my future would like if Dad didn't get better.

Pausing here, just as I did in the first chapter, remember when I said *my family didn't get off to a great start?* Several years passed since standing upon my chair in 1983 to this point in my story, fourteen years to be exact. I think it's safe to say, my family was *still* in a rough patch. It was while writing these last few chapters that I felt conflicted stringing together consecutive miserable stories while trying to communicate to **you**, a message of hope. I wanted to write, "But wait, it gets better," when in fact, it didn't get better. But this is *real* life.

I'm sure you can relate to this type of season, a time in your life when the bad news and trials kept compounding. Maybe the old saying, "When it rains it pours," is a quote you feel in your bones. The toughest seasons in life are when we experience the greatest change, good or bad. A season of despair is capable of turning our whole lives upside down and crushing every optimistic, hopeful thought along the way. I know this because as you have read, I walked through several rough storms, sometimes contemplating whether life itself was worth living. Why embark on a path that seems to get worse with every step? (*That's a hopeless mindset.*)

I'm no stranger to fear and pain, but I choose to be stronger than them. I interact with people every day who share their fears and concerns with me. Fear of failure, rejection, and humiliation have such overwhelming control on people's lives that it stops them from pursuing the life they dream about. Pain has similar effects on people. Our pain can feel so strong it consumes our thoughts and makes us narrowly focus on our ache. Every human will experience failure, loss, and countless moments of disappointment and hurt—it *cannot* be escaped. I don't know what season you are in right now. Maybe life is full of sunshine and going wonderfully for you, or maybe you're neck deep in a mudhole, doubting you'll ever escape. Those are two extremes. Maybe you're somewhere in between, but wherever you are, you have the freedom to choose your reactions. How you respond to every changing season in life says a lot about who you are as a person. I'll be the first to admit that I haven't always been proud of my reactions and responses in life, but I am grateful for the way they've shown me how to be better. I'm always learning.

I struggled navigating the painful events of my childhood. I wanted a guide for every single step– a structured plan to lead me through the storm. Mama couldn't take all my hurt away and her time with me was short lived; but I'll never forget her reminding me to be strong and to have hope in my future, whether or not I understood it. When she was gone, and her voice no longer filled the walls of our home or my listening ears, I was left to make a daily choice—to live a strong life or act like a victim and give up.

It's safe to say, a lot of us give up too soon. At the first sight of discomfort or letdown, we throw in the towel and assume we are on the wrong path or maybe we aren't capable of overcoming. I'm not sure how we were led to believe that the hard things in life are impossible mountains to climb, but it would be wise if we start looking at those enormous mountains and start climbing them— it's *how* we get stronger. Life's challenges weren't meant to devalue and shame you; no, all those hard things are meant to carve you into the powerful human you were *always* meant to be. I was lucky to have an incredible woman come into my life during my senior year in high school, Liz. She was around the same age as Mama and she worked on the school campus during lunch. Her loving kindness and intentional conversations helped me to continue pursuing a soccer scholarship after I told her I had decided to stay home and work two jobs after I graduated. She reminded me, "Sally, your Mama would be so sad to know that you gave up on your dreams. I know it's hard right now, but I can help you." Liz was my guide in those dark months and reminded me that it was okay to not understand where my life was headed or how soccer would play out in my life. I just needed to keep going; to keep putting one foot in front of the other. Like Mama, Liz was an encourager- a constant reminder of hope; and someone who I feel wonderfully indebted to, to this day.

When I won Badwater 135 in 2021, I did not feel strong and triumphant. I spent most of the 135 miles dealing with diarrhea amid the volcanic heat that seemed hotter than years past. I lost count of the number of times I was forced to stop because of my revolting intestines. The rapidly increasing fatigue I experienced because I was unable to keep nutrition down, weighed on me like a bag of cement. My crew—Colin Cooley, Dave Daley, Sarah Attar, and Eddie(my husband)—knew I was battling, but I held most of my thoughts inside knowing that complaining served no purpose. I planned to talk myself through those dark moments and had specific positive words to remind myself that no matter how hard it got, I would give my best. But something nudged at me as I made my way up Mount Whitney Portal Road (the final twelve mile, 5,000-foot climb) in the middle of the night. Maybe it was when I realized how much time I had lost stopping every forty-five minutes to go to the bathroom. I had missed my time goal, and it hurt. Even though I was in first place, it wasn't in the way I *wanted* it to be. Has this happened to you? You work with all your heart toward a goal and when you're in it; and it's different than how you envisioned it, you negatively view it as bad or disappointing? Real life is filled with these moments and even when things are not the way we hoped them to be, when we bravely step forward and embrace the moment just as it is, we open the floodgates of possibility and growth. The best things in life beckon us to push through the hard stuff- to never quit. What we want and what we need will rarely agree; but maybe that's one of the secret ingredients to achieving a goal: We embrace everything, the highs and the lows, knowing it will all work out for the good. Courageously standing in *every* season of life is how we reach the summits of our one, precious life.

Two miles from the Badwater 135 finish line, I paused and rested my hands on my knees. The stabbing pain in my calf that began four hours prior was now causing me to hobble, and the nausea made my entire torso curl inward. I was steps away from the crew car and Eddie jogged over to check on me, "You're doing amazing! You're almost there!"

I took a few deep breaths and then responded, "I can't believe I missed my time goal. Look at me, I'm moving so slow and I feel so damn weak." Tears of exhaustion and frustration filled my eyes as I achingly straightened up.

I took a few steps and Eddie stayed next to me, "Are you kidding? I've watched you push through so much! You were strong all day Sally . . . you have always been strong."

I turned eighteen two weeks before Dad was arrested. It was the end of my senior year in high school and I was rehearsing on stage for our annual school play. Over a hundred students made up the cast and crew, and a group of us had just stepped on stage to practice a singing and dancing part in preparation for opening night.

The memory of the sanctuary where we rehearsed is vivid in my mind. I remember the soft glow of the lights and the sound of giggling students huddled in the pews, waiting for their turn to take the stage. At the center of it all stood Lana, the director, with her clipboard in hand and her burgundy hair tied half-up. I was standing on stage, waiting for the music to begin, when suddenly the room was thrown into chaos by an abrupt commotion. Confused, I turned to the director, who motioned for the music to stop. A chill ran down my spine as I saw students pointing frantically at the full-length windows on the other side of the room. I looked to where they were pointing and froze in horror—it was *my* dad!

Dad was handcuffed, walking between two police officers. Within seconds, the entire room searched for me, hundreds of eyes stared as whispers moved like dominoes through the rows of students. I was exposed, and there was nowhere for me to hide. I shot a side-glance to my friend group sitting in the fourth row. They looked shocked and confused.

Lana called to me—I ran down the stage steps and awkwardly grabbed my backpack, still feeling everyone's eyes on me. I imagined this was the first time most of those students had seen someone arrested up close, and to know that the person being arrested was connected to me, was undoubtedly fascinating. Within moments, I went from acting on stage to a real life circus act. No doubt they recalled, *Wasn't this the same girl who just lost her mom to cancer?*

As I got closer to Lana, she whispered, "Sweetie, you need to go outside. There are a few police officers who want to talk with you."

I hoped the cops waiting for me would be the same kind police officers who visited me at the coffeehouse every Saturday afternoon. I typically worked alone and these two nice cops routinely came by and checked on me. I always made them mochas and warmed up chocolate chip muffins while we chatted. They knew a little about my story and how Mama had just died. I needed someone who knew me to stand with me at that moment. But when I stepped outside, two unfamiliar faces greeted me, and one of them asked, "Hello, are you, Sally?" I felt small next to their tall frames and glanced at both of their serious faces, "Yes, that's me."

My body temperature dropped as we stood in the shade next to the courtyard. The courtyard was a high traffic area, and I wished we were hidden in a room so that every person who walked by wouldn't stare at me. I was already angry Dad was arrested in a painfully public way. Why couldn't they have taken him away in the back parking lot? Why did they have to arrest him in front of the entire school?

I stood, frozen in place, as they explained they were arresting Dad for child abuse. They handed me a clipboard and said my sisters were going to live in a children's home while they further investigated the situation. Panic-stricken, I asked questions about my sisters, "For how long? Where are they going? I'm eighteen. Can I be their guardian?"

The police officers shook their heads and explained that because I still lived at home where Dad would eventually be released, I could not care for my sisters there. Not wanting to accept their response, I begged, "Please, what can I do? I told my Mom I would look out for them. You can't just take them away! Wait, where are they now?"

Sensing my worry, the police officers attempted to comfort me, "They'll be in good hands, Sally. Your sisters are already on their way, but we are aware you have an older brother so they might be able to stay with him. Either way, we'll make sure someone contacts you when you have been cleared as a guardian."

Irrepressible sadness settled in. If it were possible for a human to crumble into dust like Mama did in my nightmares, then this would be the moment it happened. I thought of my sisters and how I didn't get to say good-bye. I pictured their scared faces as strangers with badges walked them toward a mysterious car and took them away.

I looked down at the clipboard in my hands. It felt heavy. And then the police officer explained, "Sally, if you can relay any information about your dad that would be helpful to us." I thought of Dad in the back of the police car and felt sorry for him. *He's so sick. Don't they know how sick he is?*

My mind played tricks on me as I fumbled with the pen and then the monster's face appeared. He leaned toward me and growled, "I'm not an abuser, Sally! I was teaching you a lesson! You DESERVED every punishment you got from me.

That's what parents are supposed to do!" The monster roared as I scribbled on the few lines allotted for me to write, "You liar! How dare you make up stories about me!" Anxious, I stopped writing and gave the clipboard back to the cops.

After exchanging a few more words, we parted ways, and I ran to my car and drove straight home. As I pulled into the driveway, I realized for the first time in my life, I was walking into an empty house—no parents, no siblings, just me. I threw open the front door and hurled my backpack across the living room and shouted into the ceiling, "What do you want? I have NOTHING! You took *everyone* away! WHY, GOD? WHY?"

I dropped onto the wooden floor and curled into a ball. I was alone, and the loneliness ached down to the marrow of my bones. The faces of everyone in my family raced through my mind and then, like vapor, disappeared.

I could have handled getting an *F* on a test, being fired from one of my jobs, or even breaking an ankle during a soccer game— you know, normal teenage stuff. Most of what I experienced had an extreme element to it, always dramatic and polarizing. When teenagers broke a bone, their friends signed their cast or played around with their crutches during lunch break. It was a common setback. I wasn't about to kick my feet up during a sleepover with my best girlfriends and talk about death, tumors, and handcuffs. My setbacks isolated me.

I rolled onto my back and cried until the sun went down. The living room was dark and not a single light in the house had been turned on. Only the glow from the green digital clock on the CD player cast light in the room. I stared at the brightness and watched the time change. It was impossible not to think of Mama when I was alone. I squinted my eyes at the ceiling as warm tears streamed down my cheeks, and whispered, "I miss you so much. I wish I was with you."

I thought about the intense pain Mama had endured in the last months of her life. I hated how long she battled cancer and the way it stripped her to skin and bones. But she didn't give up like I wanted to. Mama pushed through all the hard parts and even though she looked weak, she made it to *her* finish line.

Have you ever stood at the finish line of a race? It's one of my favorite places to be when I'm not competing. No matter if the athlete is in first or last place, the facial expressions are what I'm watching. At some point in my spectating, tears well up in my eyes as I watch a runner so moved by the sheer vision of the words "FINISH" their whole demeanor changes. Suddenly, their torso that was hunched in fatigue straightens and their pace quickens. A renewed energy mysteriously rushes through their body—the kind we can only tap into when we believe in ourselves. Can you hear the runner? "I'm gonna do it . . . there's the Finish! Just a few more steps!" The finish line is a symbol of accomplishment and for many runners, brings a sense of relief as they realize whatever battle or discomfort they experienced on the race course is now done- the journey has come to an end; and the prize is theirs to hold.

As someone who's loved running since I was a child, I frequently envision myself winning a big race and in my mind, being strong for every mile. When I picture myself nearing the finish, I imagine my body powerfully striding through those final steps and victoriously breaking the tape with my arms reaching overhead. I always want that perfect finish line photo— one that's an image of triumph and strength. I suppose the child in me came out as I neared the Badwater finish line. I wanted that strong performance that ended in a powerful finish.

In my deep fatigue at Badwater 135 I forgot the most valuable lessons I knew to be true. Being strong wasn't about how smooth my performance was, it was about how I responded to every setback along the course. I could choose to be strong and still have a limp, and I could win despite a rough journey. Unknown to me at the time, winning Badwater 135 after battling setback after setback was the truest reflection of who I am. I didn't win because I had a perfectly executed race, and I didn't win because I was better than anyone else. I won because I chose to keep going despite the setbacks. I believed in myself and released what I couldn't control; and I kept hope at the forefront of every step. When things got especially uncomfortable, I gave myself *one* choice. Choose to be strong or choose to give up.

As I lay on the floor in my house, I closed my eyes and tried to remember the sound of Mama's voice. Those last meaningful conversations had impacted me in ways I didn't know words were capable of doing. I focused on the truth in her words. The truth, that life was going to get really hard. She was right. I didn't know what was happening to my sisters, but the thought of their precious faces made me turn outward. I released the tension in my hands and wiped my face with the edge of my t-shirt. Feeling for the ground beneath me, I pushed up to a seated position and leaned against the wall. Drawing my knees to my chest, I closed my eyes and pictured Mama's face speaking to me on my seventeenth birthday, "You ARE strong . . . you're gonna be okay."

I thought about Mama standing sickly in the rain, and an image of her frail arms reaching for me the night before she died. *She chose to be strong.*

Mama was strong in **hope** for her children,
Strong in **belief** for the strength inside her,
And strong in **love** for the life given to her.
I had one choice to make.
I could choose to be strong or
I could choose to give up.
I wearily stood up in that room where Mama died,

And I chose strong because if Mama could do it in the face of death,

I, too, could do it with the abundance of life in my chest.
I chose strong that day
And I've chosen *strong* ever since.
It was the choice that changed everything.

#CHOOSESTRONG

CHILDHOOD PHOTOS

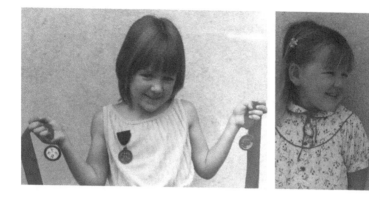

Seven years old and the start
of my medal collection

Four

Boy

Work Hard. Be Hard (Luggin
beer to a soccer party.)

9 years old. Cute and ready
for a ball to the face.

(15 yrs.old) Always
smiling at school,
but on picture
day, Mama was
at the hospital.
Smiling was hard
on this day.

1km felt like a long race back then.

High School Soccer

Electrical Man

My Beautiful Mama

(13) Mama usually took our school photos. Twin Peaks, CA

A yellow flower in my hair- Hanging out with Danielle and Bonnie.

Mama (early 1970s)

Stay curious.

The Balance Beam

Last picture together beneath the willow tree.

EPILOGUE

My sisters eventually returned home after nine months of being moved to various homes, sometimes they were kept together and sometimes they were separated. Dad only spent a few days in jail and was then ordered to attend meetings to work on his anger.

Two weeks after Dad was arrested, I graduated from high school and with the enormous help of my mom friend, Elizabeth, I sought out a scholarship at local universities. Less than three months before the college semester started, I was awarded a soccer scholarship to Biola University where I met my best friend and now husband, Eddie McRae.

I lived at Biola University for four years which was only a 40 minute drive from home. During that time, I maintained two jobs while taking a full class schedule of eighteen units each semester. As a starter and eventual captain of the women's soccer team, I continued learning how to juggle a busy schedule, often functioning on only four hours of sleep.

Dad is still alive today. I have forgiven him and hope for nothing but good and love for his life. After many years of trying to establish some type of real and healthy relationship with him, we continued having difficulties. The panic and anxiety I continually experienced before and after being around him began to negatively affect my mental health as well as my family. Forgiving and loving Dad from afar has allowed me to be a present wife and mother. I have learned that regardless if others deny us or don't ask for forgiveness, we can still forgive. Forgiving Dad helped me see my great need for forgiveness, too. I am flawed and imperfect, but through forgiveness, I can freely let go of hurt and bitterness.

The above details and their full and insightful stories are being written in Book 2 of my memoir series. Additionally, the next book tells how I went from pursuing a soccer career to becoming a professional ultra runner as a young mother, which is a commonly asked question. Originally, this memoir was more than fifty chapters, but after much debate, I decided to split the memoir into two parts. My first eighteen years of life laid a foundation for the woman I am today, and I wanted to focus on these stories as a way to communicate a powerful message of hope and strength.

I hope YOU believe in the strength inside you. Even in your weary seasons when you're tired and you're limping through another day, remember, this is *your* story and only *you* can live it. No matter who you are; where you are from; or what you look like; or what kind of family you were raised in, I believe your life is full of invaluable purpose.

You ARE strong.
I hope you choose to believe it,
I hope you choose to stand in it,
Unaltered and fully valid.

Your friend always,

(yellowrunner)

AFTERWORD

THE
CHOOSE STRONG
PROJECT

In July 2022, I stood at the *lowest point* in North America, *Death Valley* at Badwater Basin, 282 feet below sea level. Even at 11pm, the hellish heat pressed into our bodies as we awaited the start of the third and final wave of the Badwater 135 ultramarathon, *The Toughest Footrace on the Planet*; this was my third time on the start line. For those who have followed me on social media, over the years, I have said the Badwater Basin to Mount Whitney route holds a deeply personal meaning to me. The original Badwater course starts at the *lowest point,* travels through the fully exposed merciless desert, climbs three mountain ranges, and ends with a solid 11,000+' climb to the summit of Mount Whitney, 146 miles later. Mount Whitney is the *highest point* in the lower 48 states at 14,505 feet, towering in all its strength and beauty in the Sierra Nevada Mountain range. If it were possible for a mountain trail or running route to describe the story of my life, I would choose this one; and it's why the *Choose Strong Project* started and finished on this route.

I spent many seasons wondering if my journey would end battling cancer, and saying good-bye to my children too early. These thoughts were more common in my youth, but as I got older, I changed my perspective. *What if I did everything possible to be strong, healthy and fully alive at 43?* I knew I couldn't predict when or how my life would end, but every day, I could *choose* to live a courageous life. With the realization that 2022 would be the year I'd turn 43 years old, the same age Mama was when she lost her battle to cancer, I considered how I could celebrate the meaningful milestone but also honor Mama's powerful life. Weeks before April 30th and twenty-six years after Mama sat in her wheelchair and placed yellow gifts in my hands; I recalled her loving encouragement, and the CHOOSE STRONG PROJECT was born:

THE CHOOSE STRONG PROJECT

507 MILES

6 EVENTS

*BADWATER 135 Miles

*ANGELES CREST 101 Miles

*LEADVILLE 100 Miles

*SWITZERLAND/CRANS MONTANA 68 Miles

*MOUNT WHITNEY DOUBLE SUMMIT 92 Miles

*HOME TO GRAVESIDE 11 Miles

START DATE: JULY 1TH

END DATE: SEPTEMBER 30TH

For every month Mama got to live, I ran one mile, to total 507 miles. Each event was specifically chosen to represent the challenging parts of not only my story, but Mama's story. Additionally, I purposely picked races that were scheduled close together so that on race day, my body would *not* be fully recovered; I would begin each race weary. This is *not* something I recommend, nor coach people to do when training for a race, but with over 20 years of endurance running on my legs and almost 30 years spent lifting weights, I believed I could handle the intensity it would undoubtedly bring me. My mind was not focused on racing, setting personal bests or holding a medal in my hands; my mind was focused on enduring every step as a way to tell a story and to connect and encourage others along the way. The fatigue, and mental struggles in the races would be gentle metaphors to the real life experiences I have known. I knew the project would be hard, but I believed whole-heartedly that I would complete every step, no matter the circumstance.

If you're interested in watching the full CHOOSE STRONG FILM, you can view it for free on YouTube. Also, be sure to listen to all the Choose Strong Project episodes where we chronicle each event and share insightful, entertaining stories. My podcast, the CHOOSE STRONG PODCAST is available on all major podcast platforms.

#choosestrong

ACKNOWLEDGEMENTS

I hesitate to add this page as my gratitude for those who have encouraged me to keep writing this book is endless- I know there are a pile of names I will have forgotten (thankfully there is a second book coming in this memoir series.) To my precious family and friends who have shown so much love toward me, thank you.

Eddie, my redwood tree, thank you for unconditionally loving me in every season of my life. This book would have never been published without you- thank you for your endearing encouragement to never give up. You are gold.

My Makenzie and Isaiah, writing your names in my book brought tears to my eyes several times. You are and always will be the greatest blessings I have ever known. Thank you for always asking about the progress on my book; hugging me and giving me words of love on the hard days; and filling our home with joy and laughter. May you always know you are deeply loved; full of purpose; and overflowing with strength. I believe in you...always have, always will. Xoxo

The whole McRae Family and Jim and Sue thank you for all your support and love over the years; especially for Makenzie and Isaiah- appreciate you so much. Becky, I can't remember the last time I called you my sister-in-law, thank you for being my sister and friend; you're a treasure. Mark Pesce, my broski thanks for the waves, the encouraging words; and your relentless check-ins-love you. Uncle Bob and Katy thank you for treating me like family since the first day you met me- it's meant so much to me.

My Biola buds who are basically like family- Natalie, Carrie, Jennelle, Kendra, Michele, Becky, Leslie, Jamie, Nick, Kyle, Jason, Steve, Jonathan, Steve, Tommy, Andy. My life has been full of the best memories, laughter, and encouragement because of you. I love you guys so much and look forward to the many years ahead. Seriously who has the SC? =)

Liz- my angel; you were put in my life during my darkest times. You are and always will be so precious to me- miss you.

Scott and Kerry- You gotta try this cheese. Tall coffee? Both of you have changed my life; my perspective; and have lovingly shown me what it means to live a full and courageous life. I thank God for you daily.

The BPN team- Nick, Stef, Tony, A-Rod, Tyler, Drew, Adam, Jordan, Kat, Austin, and so many others who know my story; believe in me; and have supported the Choose Strong story from day one. Your support has meant the world to me.

Nick Bare and Brian Mazza- two of the very few men who were bold enough to let me tell my story and share my message on your platforms.

Colin and Dave- There should be awards for the most enduring crew and pacers because you would win the category by a landslide. Thank you Colin for changing my perspective on Mount Baden Powell over a decade ago and encouraging me to keep going and then pushing me toward countless finish lines. Dave, your gentleness and kindness during some of the lowest points in training and racing helped me to keep going when I didn't believe I could. I love you both like brothers and will be forever grateful for the hundreds of incredible memories we've had together- cheers to many more.

Kristin, I still remember the day I met you and the green smoothie you placed in my hands. You are a kind and selfless friend and the runs we have shared together will always be some of my favorites. Grateful the book is done so we can see each other more.

Jason, Adam, and Brandon, my favorite men in North Carolina. Three incredible fathers and leaders. Your families are so blessed by you. Thank you for the many years of adventurous runs, trail camps, belly-aching laughter and real conversations. Those memories will forever be gold to me, as will you.

My HB Mamas- it takes a village to raise children and I am continually grateful for you and the way you have loved and supported my babes over the years. You are all incredible mamas.

Adam W.- for years you encouraged me to keep writing. It finally happened; and I can't thank you enough.

Coach Kerk- I don't think there was a single session where I didn't feel empowered. Thank you for your guidance, optimism, hilarious banter and overall belief in me. You're incredible at what you do.

Slater and Mo-Mo- dirt, renovations, trails, and the best conversations; love you guys! Family for life- Let's shred!

Karen, Jen, Eileen, and Jill- I think of you often; wished you lived next door; and hope to see you soon. Thank you for your overwhelming love and support over the years.

Emma D- I hope you always know how precious you are. Thank you for always being a friend to me.

Susan, Rose and Daisy- Thank you for being incredible friends to my Mama; she loved you so much.

My siblings- I love you more than I could ever express. May you always believe that you are valued, strong, and worthy of true, unconditional love.

CONNECT AND JOIN THE CHOOSE STRONG COMMUNITY!

https://linktr.ee/yellowrunner

CHOOSE STRONG

CONNECT WITH ME!
→

LISTEN TO THE CHOOSE STRONG PODCAST

WATCH THE CHOOSE STRONG FILM

JOIN THE SALLY MCRAE STRENGTH APP

SUBSCRIBE TO THE SALLY MCRAE
YOUTUBE CHANNEL

FOLLOW SALLY MCRAE ON INSTAGRAM

ABOUT THE AUTHOR

Sally McRae is an American professional mountain runner and champion of the Toughest Footrace on the Planet, Badwater 135. As part of her Choose Strong message, Sally attempted a 92 mile route to become the first person to double summit Mount Whitney from Lone Pine, California in a single attempt. McRae has competed in over 60 ultramarathons, often standing on podiums all over the world. Known for her mental fortitude, Sally is a highly sought after speaker and coach who has traveled around the world sharing her powerful story and inspiring people of all ages and walks of life for over 20 years. A proud mother of two and wife, Sally resides in Southern California where she regularly trains in the San Gabriel Mountains.